A MATTER OF BALANCE

PERSONAL STRATEGIES
FOR ALCOHOL AND OTHER DRUGS

A PREVENTION WORKBOOK

by

Michael E. Holstein, Ph.D.
William E. Cohen
Paul J. Steinbroner

Book Design by Linda S. Sturgeon

CNS Publications, Inc.

CNS PUBLICATIONS, INC.

P.O. Box 96
130 3rd Street
Ashland, OR 97520
Tel: (503) 488-2805
Fax: (503) 482-9252

A MATTER OF BALANCE, FIRST EDITION

© 1995 Michael E. Holstein, William E. Cohen, Paul J. Steinbroner

ISBN 0-926544-12-8
Printed in the U.S.A.

INTRODUCTION

Prevention is where science and hope meet to make a promise. The promise of prevention is that individuals have the ability to protect themselves by reducing risk and avoiding harm. Each person is the author of her or his destiny. The choices that one makes and the experiences that one has provide the protection and resiliency to safely live one's life story. This book blends information and exercises to provide the tools for you to develop health sustaining skills and strategies for living in a world where alcohol, tobacco, medicines, and other drugs are plentiful. Every reader, from abstainer to addict, will find value and support within these pages. Go in health.

Michael P. Haines. Ph.D., Coordinator
Health Enhancement Services
Northern Illinois University

ACKNOWLEDGMENTS

We owe debts of thanks and gratitude to those who helped us with this book.

Professional Reviewers:
    Dana De Witt, Ph.D., Department of Criminal Justice, Chadron State College; **Martha FitzGerald, MN, FNP,** Jackson County Health Department; **Gerald Garrett, Ph.D.,** Department of Sociology, University of Massachusetts; **Michael P. Haines, Ph.D.,** Health Enhancement Services, Northern Illinois University; **Darryl Inaba, Pharm.D.,** Director, Haight-Ashbury Training, Education, and Aftercare Project; **Jerome Witheril, Ph.D.,** Department of Safety Studies, University of Wisconsin-Whitewater.

Special thanks to:
    Jim Brown, Southern Oregon State College Publications Office; **Rev. Ray Finerty, O.P.,** The Newman Center, SOSC; **Ron Johnson,** Executive Director National Family Life and Education Center, Los Angeles; **Cheryl Presley, Ph.D.,** Student Health, University of Illinois, Carbondale; **Betty Redleaf, Ph.D.,** Director of Student Support Services, Nebraska Indian Community College; **Louise Stanger, MSW,** Department of Social Work, San Diego State University; **The Trauma Foundation** at San Francisco General Hospital.

Student Reviewers:
    Ashleigh Adams, Justin Adams, Sarah Steenhuis.

We are also grateful to:
    Carol Caruso, CNS Productions, Inc; **Joan Jackson,** Associate Dean, Southern Oregon State College; **Jan Janssen,** Youth Diversion Officer, Ashland Police Department, Ashland, Oregon.

The merits of **A Matter of Balance** derive from their generous guidance and counsel. Its flaws are our own.
—MEH, WEC, PJS

TO THE TEACHER

Knowledge about drugs provides an important foundation for drug abuse prevention. But knowledge-only courses risk encouraging passivity and indifference ("So what?"), self-distancing ("All this doesn't apply to me"), self-inoculation ("I can handle it"), or resignation ("I can't do anything about it anyway").

A MATTER OF BALANCE is intended for courses in substance abuse, health and wellness, and counseling, as well as for programs in athletics, peer advising, and for other situations where personalized, interactive, drug awareness and drug abuse prevention skills are desirable. A MATTER OF BALANCE might also be used in courses such as "The First-Year Experience," "Introduction to College Life," or in a similar "surviving college" course, especially since the first year is where heavy risk occurs. This workbook can stand alone as a course text or serve as a hands-on activities workbook to supplement other course textbooks. It can also be used in DUI and DWI courses, workshops, and in at-risk and probationary programs.

We offer practical applications, skill-building exercises, chances to think critically about issues, and specific activities to practice and apply to the students' own situations. Our workbook covers abstention and limited use by focusing on self-assessment, stress reduction, natural highs, refusal skills, self-esteem, and models for change. It also leads students through strategies for harm reduction and self-protection when controlling use is the goal. When intervention and treatment are called for, it suggests a series of first steps.

A MATTER OF BALANCE encourages students to think personally and critically about alcohol and other drug issues by introducing them on the first page of every 4-page chapter. These provide the basis for the following kinds of exercises and activities.

FYI's provide brief additional information on chapter topics.

Workbook Exercises, which are detachable, include self-reflection, personal applications, and skill-building exercises. Because there are no right or wrong answers to these, we see the Workbook Exercises as additional opportunities to learn.

Group Exercises, which include both small and large group activities, offer students opportunities to share and compare knowledge and values, to role play, to collaborate, and essentially to learn from and contribute to one another.

Personal Inquiries are prompts for personal diary entries to be made in the back of the workbook.

Teaching prevention involves many skills: addressing a wide spectrum of experience and attitude, communicating credible information, and above all, creating a safe, accepting environment in which students determine the tone and direction of the discussion. As Galileo said, "You cannot teach someone anything. You can only help them to discover it within themselves."

TABLE OF CONTENTS

Interchapter III: Halting the Progression 90

TO THE STUDENT

A MATTER OF BALANCE will help you examine your attitudes and practices with regard to alcohol and other drugs. It will deepen your understanding of substance abuse issues and ask you to draw on your own knowledge and experience to explore questions involving substance abuse. It will also ask you to practice activities that may broaden your understanding of why people abstain from using alcohol and other psychoactive drugs, how people limit their use and reduce harm, how substance abuse can become a problem, and how people can help or get help when substance abuse does become a problem.

ORGANIZATION OF THIS WORKBOOK

Alcohol and Other Drug Topics are introduced on the first page of every 4-page chapter. These provide the basis for the following kinds of exercises and activities.

FYI's furnish additional facts or perspectives on chapter subjects.

Workbook Exercises, included on the second and third page of each chapter, ask you to write about various aspects of the topic. These pages are detachable, and you may be asked to turn them in.

Group Exercises appear on the fourth and final page. These involve subjects for small and large group activities and discussion.

Personal Inquiries at the very end of the chapter provide suggestions for entries in a personal journal at the back of the book.

We have written this workbook with the following ideas in mind:

■ Experiential learning is a necessary supplement to conceptual and factual learning.
■ You can use the tools presented in this workbook to help you shape your future to whatever degree you wish.
■ Some readers of the book won't ever drink or use, some don't use now but may later, some use now, while others already have problems with alcohol and other drugs. Whatever relationship you may or may not have with alcohol and other drugs, there is something valuable in this book for you.
■ You are at a point in your life where you are responsible for your own well-being. You are the author of your own future. This workbook will enable you to try on different ideas and feelings and contrast them with those of other people.

DISCLAIMER: Information and activities in this book are in no way meant to replace professional counseling and treatment.

THE FAR SIDE

By GARY LARSON

9-15 Larson © Chronicle Features, 1983

"I don't like this . . . The carnivores have been boozing it up at the punchbowl all night — drinking, looking around, drinking, looking around . . ."

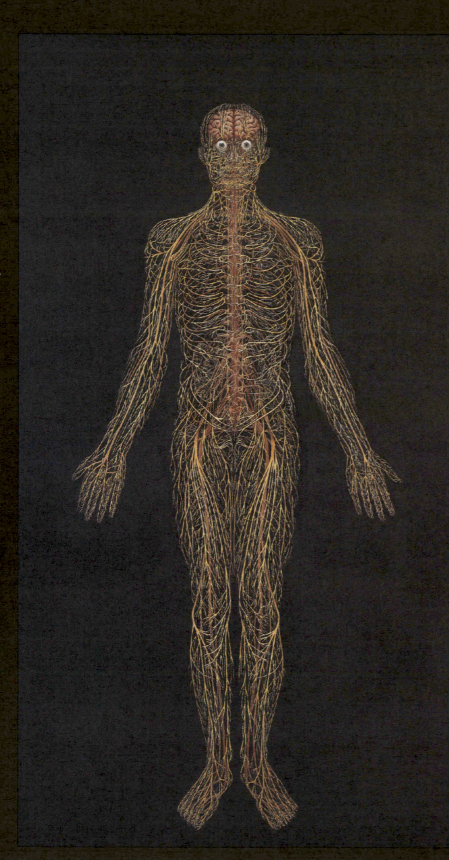

Nervous System © 1979 Alex Grey

Psychoactive drugs are natural or synthetic substances such as alcohol, cocaine, LSD, tobacco, and marijuana which have significant effects on the brain and spinal cord (central nervous system). These substances manipulate brain chemicals which in turn cause emotional, mental, and physical effects.

The choice to use alcohol and other drugs, the level of involvement, and the risk of developing problems is governed by 3 factors: heredity, environment, and psychoactive drugs.

Heredity gives us our starting point in life. The genes we inherit from our parents determine many physical and mental characteristics, including the initial make-up of our nervous system. They can also determine our susceptibility or resistance to excessive drug use.

Our **environment**, particularly the emotional and physical pressures of childhood, then moderates or distorts many hereditary traits and teaches us how to act and react to life and to the appeal of psychoactive drugs. These changes are recorded by alterations in our nervous system.

Finally, the choice to use and the level of involvement is determined by **psychoactive drugs** themselves. These substances, by their very nature, can rewire parts of our central nervous system, changing the way we act and react to the people around us and to our surroundings, thereby increasing or decreasing our control over the use of psychoactive drugs.

CLASSIFICATION

The 3 main groups of psychoactive drugs are uppers (stimulants), downers (depressants), and all arounders (psychedelics).

UPPERS: Stimulants include cocaine ("crack," "coke," "snow"), amphetamines and methamphetamines ("crank," "speed," "ice," diet pills), nicotine, and caffeine.

Stimulants initially cause an increase in heart rate and blood pressure; the stronger stimulants energize muscles, decrease appetite, cause some mental and physical alertness, give a feeling of confidence, and induce some euphoria. Excess amounts can cause insomnia, extremely high blood pressure, and heart and blood vessel problems, particularly if the user has a sensitivity to the drug. Extended use often causes irritability, anxiety, mental confusion, paranoia, exhaustion, some violence, and dependency.

DOWNERS: Depressants are divided into 3 general categories: **Alcohol** which includes wine (and wine coolers), beer (and light beer), and hard liquor such as whiskey, rum, vodka, gin, and tequila. **Opiates** include morphine, heroin, codeine, methadone, Demerol, and Darvon. **Sedative-hypnotics** include Xanax, Valium, Halcion, phenobarbital, and seconal.

Generally, small doses of downers depress respiration, heart rate, and reaction time; relax muscles, and subdue physical and/or mental pain; lower inhibitions; produce sedation; and initially, induce different levels of euphoria. Opiates can also decrease muscular coordination and energy and cause constipation, nausea, depression, physical dependence, and withdrawal symptoms if used to excess. They can also cause overdoses.

ALL AROUNDERS: These **psychedelics** which include marijuana, LSD, peyote, psilocybin mushrooms, MDMA ("ecstasy"), and PCP can stimulate or depress us physically, but the mental and emotional effects are more pronounced. They can distort the way the brain interprets sensory information. They can also mimic certain mental illnesses.

OTHER psychoactive drugs include: **inhalants** (e.g., airplane glue, laughing gas, gasoline, and "poppers" or nitrites); **psychiatric medications** (e.g., Prozac or Lithium) used to treat depression or other mental illnesses; **anabolic steroids** (e.g., male hormones) used to build muscles and strength; **over-the-counter medications** (e.g., diet-aids, antihistamines, and mild pain killers).

CHAPTERS 1-10 OVERVIEW

Chapters 1-10 examine personal values and attitudes towards alcohol and drug use and the associated risks in light of heredity (family history), environment (family, neighborhood, and contemporary society), and the psychological and physical changes involved with psychoactive substances and then present topics that can help you make your own choices and develop your own strategies regarding alcohol and other drugs.

Chapter 1 helps clarify your own ideas and feelings towards alcohol and other drugs and samples the attitudes of others in your group. **Chapter 2** surveys the various risks associated with the use of psychoactive drugs. **Chapter 3** uses family history (heredity) as a way of perceiving inherited tendencies that either predispose a person for problems with alcohol and other drugs or builds resiliency and strength. **Chapter 4** examines environmental pressures that can increase susceptibility for alcohol and other drug abuse such as those found on many college campuses. **Chapter 5** summarizes the neurochemical processes induced by the use of psychoactive drugs and examines the levels of use of these substances from experimentation and social use to habituation, abuse and addiction.

The next 4 chapters offer ways of enhancing one's strengths and potential. **Chapter 6** lets the reader explore natural highs, i.e., non-drug, life-affirming experiences. **Chapter 7** shows the relationship between physical health and psychoactive drugs. **Chapter 8** introduces the concept of wellness to include intellectual, emotional, spiritual, and social health. **Chapter 9** sums up the positive attributes of a person and encourages the maintenance of high self-esteem. Finally, **Chapter 10** offers a model for change as a way to solve problems, enhance strengths, or correct problems.

Handwriting On The Wall
Attitude And Values Clarification

This chapter will help you clarify your own ideas and feelings towards
alcohol and other drugs and sample the
attitudes of others.

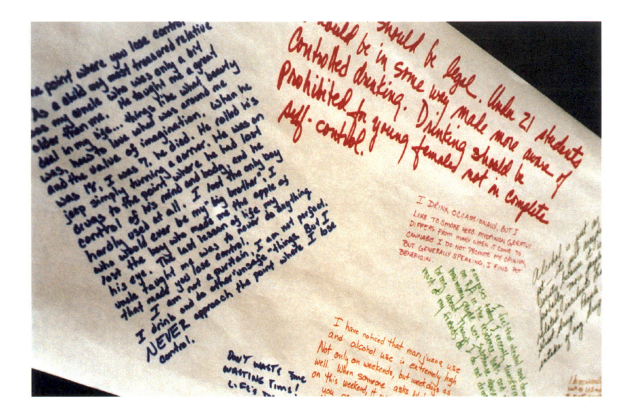

In almost every randomly selected group, there are people who run the gamut of alcohol and other drug experience from non-use, experimentation, and social use, to abuse, addiction, treatment, and recovery. There are drug naive people and drug aware people; people who support absolute prohibition of psychoactive drugs; people who argue for their complete legalization; and all shades of opinion in between.

Whatever our experience with alcohol and other drugs and our attitudes towards them, we all face issues of use and abuse either in our personal lives, in our families,

social lives, school, workplace, or in society at large.

Our starting point in this book is to help you explore both your values, the principles or standards you live by, and your attitudes regarding use of alcohol and other psychoactive drugs (those substances that chemically modify the mind and alter moods). This and following chapters will help you decide whether your practices regarding psychoactive substances are congruent with your values and attitudes, that is, with who you are and who you want to be.

FYI Socrates said, "Know thyself." Self-knowledge is the beginning of all knowledge. Knowing who you are and knowing your attitudes towards alcohol and other drugs are essential first steps in understanding and either avoiding or managing risks associated with psychoactive drugs.

Workbook Exercise 1: Consider the following set of social dilemmas and describe what you would do and why.

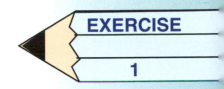

1) You have a very important examination tomorrow, but you've just been invited to a party tonight.

_____

_____

_____

_____

2) You have been invited to go out drinking with a group of people you would like to get to know. You like to drink, but they have asked you to be the designated driver.

_____

_____

_____

3) You are on your campus peer review board and one of the cases involves a friend who has been cited for being drunk and disorderly in the residence hall for the second time.

_____

_____

_____

Workbook Exercise 2: Complete the following phrases:

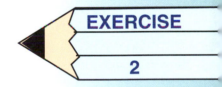

1) For most people my age, drinking is _____

_____

2) Nonsmokers should _____

_____

3) In general, drugs are _____

_____

4) If I found out my relative or friend was selling drugs, I'd _____

_____

5) A good reason (if any) for drinking is _____

_____

6) A bad reason (if any) for drinking is _____

_____

7) A good reason (if any) for taking drugs is _____

_____

8) A bad reason (if any) for taking drugs _____

_____

EXERCISE

3

Workbook Exercise 3: Skim your workbook and then summarize what you would like to learn from it.

_____

_____

_____

_____

_____

_____

_____

_____

_____

_____

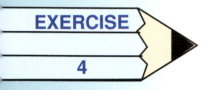

EXERCISE

4

Workbook Exercise 4: Numerically order your answers from 1: Mostly agree to 5: Mostly disagree.

1) In general, people abuse alcohol and other drugs
   ___ for pleasure
   ___ because of peer pressure
   ___ as an expression of personal freedom
   ___ to cope better
   ___ specify any other _____

2) Some people don't drink because they
   ___ can't afford it
   ___ are afraid of legal consequences
   ___ don't want to impair their health
   ___ don't understand the benefits of alcohol and other drugs
   ___ specify any other_____

3) Drunk drivers should
   ___ have their driver's license suspended for first offenses
   ___ get mandatory jail terms for first and subsequent offenses
   ___ not be given a jail term if no one is hurt
   ___ have their cars confiscated on second offenses
   ___ specify any other_____

4) The best way to solve this country's drug problems is to
   ___ legalize drugs
   ___ decriminalize or reduce penalties for possession
   ___ imprison all users
   ___ educate the public
   ___ specify any other _____

5) The greatest risk in illegal drug use is
   ___ getting caught
   ___ becoming addicted
   ___ impairing health
   ___ having supply cut off
   ___ specify any other _____

6) If my friend got drunk often, I would
   ___ not care
   ___ find a new friend
   ___ get drunk too
   ___ get the friend help
   ___ specify any other _____

Group Exercise 1: Collect your class's or group's attitudes, ideas, feelings, and experiences about alcohol, tobacco, and other drugs. Record them in 1 of 2 ways.

- Tape a length of butcher paper to the wall inside the classroom and have everyone write on it. Paper is available at a supermarket. At least a 10' length of waxed-back paper is recommended.
- If anonymity is an issue, use pieces of paper or cards and tape them up.

Afterwards, discuss
- the most typical response;
- unusual or memorable responses;
- the variety of responses;
- strikingly contrasting responses.

Group Exercise 2: Consider the issues surrounding drug education.

- Should it emphasize only abstinence or legal use? Or should it assume some level of use, legal and illegal, and seek to educate people about how to reduce harm?
- Is there too much or the wrong kind of drug education? Is there another path to take?

PI **Personal Inquiry:** Discuss the kinds of drug education you have received and whether it has had an impact on you.

CHAPTER 2

Beating The Odds
From Risk To Resiliency

Understanding and anticipating the risks associated with alcohol
and other drug use are protective strategies for
reducing risks and potential harm.

It is obvious that people get enjoyment from a psychoactive substance like alcohol.
Consumption of beer, wine, and hard liquor is too widespread and personal experiences of
favorable outcomes too common to pretend that only bad things occur when one drinks.

Euphoric Recall: The problem with alcohol and other
drugs is that people tend to remember pleasure and the
good times rather than pain and the bad times. So in
deciding whether to drink or use again, they may focus on
the buzz they got and avoid thinking about past, unpleasant side effects or any future consequences.
Unfortunately, the chemical action of alcohol and other
drugs on the brain accelerates the very process of forget-
ting negative consequences. The following factors help
determine the effects alcohol or other drugs will have on
someone who uses:

- Emotional factors include mood, expectations, previous
  experiences, and any mental problems that might exist.

- Physical factors include weight, metabolism, sex,
  health, and even the race of the user.

- External factors include the setting where the drug is
  taken and whether it is used with friends, strangers, or
  even alone.

- Another factor is polydrug use which can alter the
  action of each substance, often in unpredictable ways.
  An example of polydrug use is using alcohol to come
  down from cocaine or taking alcohol and a sedative
  together to really get loaded.

"Hey, what is this stuff? It makes everything I think seem profound."

Drawing by Warren Miller © 1978 New Yorker Magazine

- Finally, the most important factors in determining the effects alcohol or other drugs will have
  are the **amount** of the drug used, the **frequency** with which it is used, and the **period of
  time** over which it is used.

FYI Convictions for driving under the influence (DUI) or driving
while intoxicated (DWI) are part of the risk of driving after
drinking or using. Besides injuries and deaths, the cost in legal fees
and increased insurance rates can be anywhere from $4,000 to
$10,000. It is helpful to remember the concept of **0-1-3** as a rough
guide to avoiding legal trouble. This means **0** drinks if you're the designated driver, pregnant, or diabetic. If you're drinking, **1** drink an hour,
and **3** drinks in a drinking session. This should keep your blood alcohol level within the legal limit.

Workbook Exercise 1: Calculating Blood Alcohol Concentration

The key to anticipating the probable results of taking psychoactive drugs is understanding that it's not only the substance itself that causes the effects, it's the amount used in each dose or drink, how fast those doses or drinks are taken, the frequency of use over time, and whether other drugs are used at the same time. One way of determining the effects of drinks of alcohol is to calculate blood alcohol concentration.

Answer the following questions using the Blood Alcohol Concentration (BAC) table inside the back cover of this workbook.

1. To keep blood alcohol at .05 or lower, how many drinks could a person your weight and sex have? Summarize the physical effects from your experience and/or from the table.

    _____

    _____

    _____

2. What would be the blood alcohol concentration of someone your same sex and weight who had 3 drinks in 1 hour? Summarize the physical effects from your experience and/or from the table.

    _____

    _____

    _____

3. What would the blood alcohol concentration be for a person your same weight and sex who had consumed 5 drinks in 2 hours? Summarize the physical effects from your experience and/or from the table.

    _____

    _____

    _____

4. Alexi and Richard are at the same party. She weighs 125 lbs., he weighs 175 lbs. Each drinks 5 beers in 3 hours. What is the blood alcohol concentration of each as they leave the party?

    _____

| 1 1/2 oz
brandy | 1 1/2 oz liquor
w/mixer | 1 1/2 oz liquor
straight | 12 oz
beer | 7 oz malt
liquor | 5 oz wine | 10 oz wine
cooler |

Equivalency Chart: Each glass represents 1 drink.

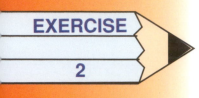

EXERCISE 2

Workbook Exercise 2: Resiliency: We all face risks and challenges in our lives. If you are at an institution of higher learning, describe which of your traits and/or sources of inner strength allowed you to overcome life's risks and challenges in order to get there.

1) _____

2) _____

3) _____

EXERCISE 3

Workbook Exercise 3: Out of every bad experience, there is usually something to be learned or something to strengthen us. Describe 3 different experiences which which were initially negative but later turned out to have positive consequences.

1) _____

2) _____

3) _____

Group Exercise 1: Wheel of Fortune: The frequency of moderate to heavy drinking sessions (moderate = 2-4 drinks per session; heavy = 5 or more drinks per session) increases the probability of negative consequences.

To help understand the risks involved, draw a wheel of fortune on the board with 16 pie-shaped slots each of which will be filled with a good or a bad effect of moderate to heavy drinking. One of the slots should have "abstain" in it. Then take suggestions from the group to fill the slots so that good effects outnumber bad effects about 3 to 1. Make sure 1 of the effects is fatal.

Select 3 players from your group to play the game. Starting at "abstain," take turns rolling 2 dice and moving around the wheel of fortune. The object is to try to get 5 good effects in a row before anybody else.

FYI An average of 4,000 Americans die from alcohol poisoning each year by drinking a large amount of alcohol in a short period of time.

"One night, when I was a freshman, I only wanted to have a couple of drinks, but after 3 shots of vodka I lost count. I woke up naked, in a hospital, with tubes in my nose and throat. The nurse said that with a .35 blood-alcohol level, I was lucky to be alive. After 11 seizures and 4 days, I was released from the hospital, but I still couldn't walk. I ended up missing 3 weeks of school. When I returned, it was mandatory that I attend AA meetings. At the end of the next semester I had to take double finals."

Tanya, a 26-year-old school teacher

PI **Personal Inquiry:** Think of the last 3 times you were drinking or with someone who was drinking. For each time, discuss whether the anticipated outcome was the actual outcome.

Shaking The Family Tree
Family Risk, Family Resiliency

Hereditary traits alone cannot cause compulsive substance use, although certain traits can increase one's susceptibility to addiction. Other hereditary factors, positive family role models, family traditions, and environmental influences can counteract risks.

Strong evidence exists for biologically inherited tendencies for alcoholism, particularly in males. There is also some evidence for inherited tendencies to abuse other drugs. There is even some evidence, although less compelling, for an inherited tendency to engage in other compulsive behaviors such as gambling or risk taking. However, **no one is destined to become an alcoholic or addict because "it runs in the family."** Heredity only endows a person with a neurochemistry more susceptible to alcohol, drugs, or the sensations caused by other compulsive behaviors.

What this means practically is that certain genes will not cause individuals to drink but can predispose them one way or the other. For example, John and Ed, are friends at college. Once John, who is genetically predisposed to alcoholism, begins drinking regularly, his progress to excessive use will be quicker than Ed's, who has no genetic predisposition. It may take Ed 10-20 years of drinking to become alcohol dependent; John may do it in a year or 2. Of course, if Ed, who has no genetic predisposition, begins drinking heavily, he can compress his progression to alcoholism into a few years. Finally, if neither Ed nor John drinks, their relative susceptibility never becomes an issue.

Being aware of your own family history is a good tool that can encourage you to exercise greater caution if there are established patterns of abuse in the family.

While family history can demonstrate risks, it can also reveal strengths: positive inherited traits, positive role models, caring and supportive relatives, healthy family traditions, and other factors that can safeguard family members, even when they come from very troubled families and grow up under the most adverse conditions.

Workbook Exercise 1: To help you better understand heredity, list any of your physical or mental traits that you feel are obviously and strongly present in a close relative.

Physical trait (e.g., hair color, body shape):

Relative(s) with a similar trait:

_____   _____

_____   _____

_____   _____

Mental trait (e.g., good memory, good with numbers):

Relative(s) with a similar trait:

_____   _____

_____   _____

_____   _____

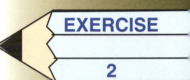

Workbook Exercise 2: It is often easy to focus on negative traits and forget the positive ones which help us survive and grow. List and then describe how 5 <u>positive</u> traits of your parents or grandparents have contributed to your character and habits.

1) _____

_____

_____

2) _____

_____

_____

3) _____

_____

_____

4) _____

_____

_____

5) _____

_____

_____

Heredity can increase an individual's susceptibility to a psychoactive substance if he or she uses that substance. Research has shown that a man who is the biological son of an alcoholic is 3 times as likely to become alcoholic than a man who is the biological son of non-alcoholics. Another study shows that if both parents and the grandfather are alcoholics, the chances of alcoholism are 9 times greater than someone with no alcoholism in his family. Still another study suggests that 1 out of 2 women with a genetic tendency to alcoholism actually becomes alcoholic. **On the other hand, 60 to 80% of people with high genetic predisposition to abuse alcohol never develop a problem**.

Workbook Exercise 3: Imagine that your father and grandfather have drinking problems. You and your brother don't drink yet. Since his and your susceptibility to overuse alcohol is high, write a letter to your brother about his liability in a manner that might keep him from beginning to drink.

_____

_____

_____

_____

_____

_____

_____

_____

_____

_____

_____

_____

_____

_____

_____

_____

_____

_____

> "My grandmother warned me, `Our family can't drink. The only exercise your grandad got was bending his elbow. Your uncle died of cirrhosis of the liver. Your aunt died of the combination of alcohol and sleeping pills. Your dad had 5 martinis every day of his business life.' I took her warning seriously (having lived through the turmoil) and, except for a brief time in the service, decided not to test my limits."
>
> 31-year-old non-drinker

Group Exercise 1: People often wonder whether they are predestined to activate inherited traits, good or bad. In small groups, discuss how individuals might be affected by behavioral traits and to what extent someone can overcome potentially negative traits or enhance positive traits. Consider such tendencies as being quick tempered, impulsive, depressed, anti-social, good humored, logical, emotional, etc. What specific steps could someone take to avoid duplicating unhealthy family tendencies and cultivating healthy ones?

Group Exercise 2: In small groups, discuss specific ways to find out about your family tree. For example, get information from the oldest member of the family. Discuss also how you can know whether relatives and ancestors have had a health, mental health, or substance abuse problem. How do you know which family members have been admirable? How do families relate or hide family history?

STURGEON

Personal Inquiry: To help you understand your family's predisposing tendencies for health problems or use of psychoactive substances, complete your family tree on page 138. If possible, note the age of each person, any health problems, and, if applicable, what each person died of. Whenever possible, include the use of any alcohol, tobacco, and other psychoactive substances on your family tree.

Turning Down
The Heat

Dealing With Your Environment

By knowing how environment can increase or lessen an individual's susceptibility to abuse psychoactive substances, you can learn to counteract negative influences and enhance positive ones.

Courtesy of SOSC Publications

Besides heredity, environmental factors, including family and community, can increase susceptibility to substance abuse. A predisposing family history might include family use, weak parenting skills, parental tolerance for deviance, and family disorganization. Risky community environments include economic and social deprivation, tolerance for illicit drug use, and easy access to drugs. (Ethnicity is a very weak predictor of substance abuse.) But even **high-risk environments do not necessarily cause a person to use drugs**. Some people have remarkable resilience and self-protective capabilities that enable them to resist strong environmental cues to use. And absolutely no one becomes alcoholic or addicted who doesn't drink or use drugs.

On the other hand, environment can also work to prevent and discourage substance abuse. Stable families with family rituals and community social supports, caring adults, non-abusing role models, including relatives, teachers, and friends all make abuse less likely. So do a non-abusing peer group, community alternatives to use, community bonding, and cultural pride.

Past environments influence us in present ones. The stronger your family's and community's resistance to substance abuse, the less likely you will be susceptible to substance abuse in a college setting. College drinking patterns may reflect or diverge from family and community drinking patterns. They also follow students' expectations as well as college traditions and the prevailing climate of opinion in our society.

FYI College campuses are high-risk environments. Various studies of college students show that

- College students do more binge drinking than their non-college counterparts.
- College traditions and customs encourage dangerous alcohol practices, such as drinking games and binge drinking (5 or more drinks in a sitting).
- College administrators believe that alcohol-related problems are involved in 40.8% of all academic problems and 28.3% of dropouts.
- College students and campuses are heavily targeted by advertising and promotions by the alcoholic beverage industry.

Workbook Exercise 1: Think about your personal assets, that is, those qualities you learned and practiced in your earlier environment, such as self-confidence. Describe 3 strengths and skills you can draw on in a college environment to keep you in control and help you avoid uninformed choices about alcohol, drugs, and other compulsive behaviors. For example, since you learned to socialize fairly easily in high school, you don't feel you must drink to be at ease with other people.

EXERCISE 1

1) Personal asset: _____

_____

_____

2) Personal asset: _____

_____

_____

3) Personal asset: _____

_____

_____

Workbook Exercise 2: Which 2 people in your earlier life helped you grow and gave you the strength to cope? How did they do it? How did they gain your trust? For example, a high school coach who inspired you to push yourself and has said to call her or him any time you want, even at college.

EXERCISE 2

1) Person: _____

How she or he helped: _____

_____

_____

2) Person: _____

How she or he helped: _____

_____

_____

EXERCISE 3

Workbook Exercise 3: Unnecessary stress is one of the major factors in a campus environment that can lead to problems with alcohol and other drugs. Stress can also damage your health. Name 4 stressors in your present life and then describe non-substance ways to counteract them. For example, one source of stress might be not getting enough sleep and becoming irritable. A solution might be deciding on a fixed bedtime or taking a daily nap.

1) Stressor:_____

   Solution:_____

   _____

   _____

   _____

   _____

2) Stressor:_____

   Solution:_____

   _____

   _____

   _____

   _____

3) Stressor:_____

   Solution:_____

   _____

   _____

   _____

   _____

4) Stressor:_____

   Solution:_____

   _____

   _____

   _____

   _____

Group Exercise 1: In small groups, discuss ways students or the administration could change the campus environment to reduce unnecessary stress.

Group Exercise 2: In small groups, share stories about methods each person has used to overcome environmental challenges, such as those caused by personal relationships, academic demands, living conditions, permissive attitudes towards risky behavior, etc.

PI **Personal Inquiry:** Write about 3 stressors from your early environment that you do or would handle differently now. For example, you used to respond to your parents yelling at you by getting out of the house. Now you are willing to face the confrontation and try to resolve the issues.

From Experimentation To Compulsion

Psychoactive Drugs

With continued use, psychoactive drugs can change one's nervous system and imprint certain behaviors. It is important to be aware of the level of psychoactive drug use at which these changes occur.

By the time we're born, heredity has given us 200 billion brain cells. By the age of 10, our environment has influenced our behavior and personality, thereby developing most of the hard wiring between nerve cells. After that, we continue learning and making more connections between our brain cells until the day we die. We can also alter that existing wiring with the use of psychoactive drugs.

Each psychoactive drug alters the chemistry of our nervous system, particularly the brain and spinal cord, in a unique way. In addition, each person reacts differently to an identical dose. One person might drink moderately for 20 years and not alter his or her chemistry to a significant degree while another, who is more susceptible because of heredity or environment, might binge just on weekends and find it difficult to control use after just 6 months. With either user, the greater the amount, frequency, and/or duration of use, the faster the changes. Ironically, it is the body's natural desire to protect itself that causes the very changes that produce the problem: tolerance, withdrawal, and craving.

- Over time, the body develops a natural resistance, called **tolerance**, to both the physical and the psychological effects of psychoactive drugs. The result is that successively higher doses of a drug are needed to get the same effect.

- If the body has changed because of excessive use, stopping use will cause the body to try to return to normal. This rebound effect will cause **withdrawal symptoms** such as a caffeine-withdrawal headache, a hangover, heroin-withdrawal sweats and body pains, or even Valium-withdrawal convulsions. In practical terms, the fear of these symptoms can keep someone using (e.g., a Bloody Mary in the morning to get rid of the shakes).

- The remembrance of pleasure, the physiological changes due to tolerance, and the fear of withdrawal symptoms can all help develop **craving** for a drug which can lead a person from experimentation, through social use, habituation, abuse, and possibly to addiction.

Workbook Exercise 1: To better understand **tolerance**, describe 2 over-the-counter or prescription medicines you have taken where continued use made the substance give less and less satisfaction or relief and made you use more for the same effect. Then describe the possible negative health consequences, and what corrective actions could be taken.
Example:

Substance: Antacids
Use pattern: Went from 2 tablets for a hot stomach to 8 a day with every meal.
Negative health consequences: Even slightly spicy foods began to cause severe heart burn after a while.
Solution: Use diet change to calm stomach, not antacids.

1) Substance: _____

   Use pattern: _____

   _____

   Negative health consequences: _____

   _____

   Solution: _____

   _____

   _____

2) Substance: _____

   Use pattern: _____

   _____

   Negative health consequences: _____

   _____

   Solution: _____

   _____

   _____

EXERCISE 1

Workbook Exercise 2: To better understand **withdrawal**, describe a substance you (or a friend) consume regularly such as tea, coffee, alcohol, soft drinks or tobacco and the use pattern. Describe the effect when use of the substance stops or is interrupted.

Substance: _____

Use pattern: _____

_____

Withdrawal effects: _____

_____

_____

EXERCISE 2

Workbook Exercise 3: To understand **craving**, describe 2 substances or activities you enjoy where doing it once or twice actually increases rather than satisfies your desire. For example, a first cigarette of the day will make a smoker want to light up another rather quickly; for some, playing a computer game once will make them want to play it for hours.

1) Substance or activity: _____

_____

_____

_____

2) Substance or activity: _____

_____

_____

_____

FYI This graph rates drugs in terms of how quickly they begin to change a person to make the progression from experimentation and social use to habituation, abuse, or addiction more likely. This is not a rating of overall danger of the drugs. It only rates the rapidity of psychological and physiological addiction based on the experience of the Haight-Ashbury Drug Clinic in San Francisco. Note that the method of use affects the speed of habituation.

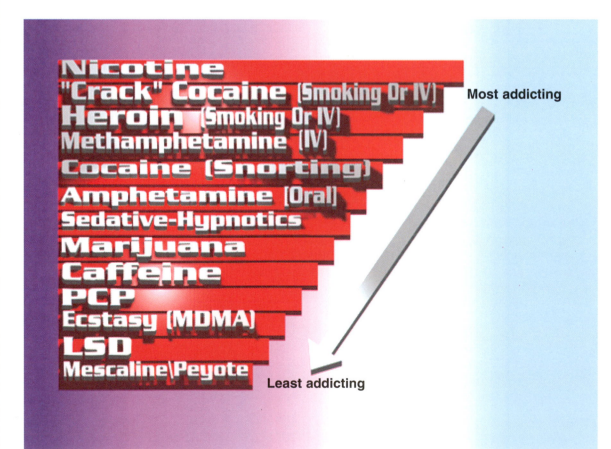

There is a progression of use of psychoactive substances that people can pass through as they use. Briefly, they are

- **Experimentation:** Alcohol or another drug is "tried out," typically on a chance basis and out of curiosity.
- **Social/recreational use:** A person seeks out the drug, but there is no established pattern; occasional health consequences.
- **Habituation:** A pattern of use exists (e.g., TGIF high, 5 cups of coffee a day). The desire to use has more control over user.
- **Drug abuse:** There is continued use despite negative consequences (e.g., high blood pressure, respiratory problems, paranoia, arrests, loss of friends, financial difficulties).
- **Addiction:** The person spends most of the time getting, using, or thinking about the drug despite serious negative health, legal, and social consequences. (A more extensive description of the different levels of use is found on pp. 90-91.)

Group Exercise 1: In small groups, discuss whether you could use the terms "experimentation," "social use," "habituation," "abuse," or "addiction" for some common behaviors such as using the Internet, buying lottery tickets, watching your favorite soap opera, or eating food on your plate in a certain order.

Group Exercise 2: In small groups, discuss what would constitute experimentation, social use, habituation, abuse, or addiction for alcohol. For example, in what category would you put someone who only got drunk on Saturday night?

Group Exercise 3: The 3 factors that determine whether a person uses drugs compulsively are heredity, environment, and psychoactive drugs. To reduce the risk of substance abuse, a person could be aware of hereditary risk factors or change his or her environment and reduce stress. In small groups, discuss what a person could do to avoid using a psychoactive drug like alcohol compulsively, that is, passing over into a level of use where the body begins to change and he or she becomes unable to control use.

Personal Inquiry: Discuss a time when using a substance or doing something either threatened to become compulsive or became compulsive and was causing you some harm (e.g., watching T.V., playing pool). What did you do or could you have done to break the pattern of use or activity?

Getting High Naturally

"The best natural high I have ever had was winning the 4A High School Football Championship Game. After the game, I was walking around watching everyone run out on the field, seeing the other team cry. I felt something that I had never felt before. I was so high I was almost seeing things that weren't really there. It felt like the stadium was surrounded by these huge white clouds and that the stadium was floating. It only lasted for about 10 minutes, but it was the best feeling I have ever had."

"A peak experience in my life was the choir competition our choir went to in Verona, Italy. The competition was the end of 6 months of practicing — 3 nights a week, every day during the holidays. I will never forget the feeling of singing with trembling, perspiring hands in front of the judges. One song, another, a third . . . I am ready to faint, my knees cannot hold my weight. Then, how hard it is to move from the stage to the dressing room, the dance and the 'Indian Prayer' after the performance, the awards ceremony. We got first place for women choirs, the award for the best performed Italian song, and the Grand Prix — practically everything possible. It felt so good being the best at least for a little while."

"For me the ultimate high is being outside. Nature, like flowers and animals, has a great influence on me. But above and beyond that, there is the sheer thrill I get from being outside on almost stormy days. The kind of day that is overcast with a hint of cold; the smell of rain, but none falling; and above all, the wind. This invigorates me. To feel the wind at my face . . . the thrill of thinking, if only for a moment, that I can fly."

"When I want a natural high, I go horseback riding. With the wind blowing through your hair, a powerful animal beneath you, there is nothing more exhilarating."

"The best high I have is during cheerleading. I have always been what they call a 'flyer,' the person who gets thrown around. I love the feeling of being thrown up into the air and when you have 1 guy who can throw and catch you with such ease, it makes you feel light. It's a great feeling."

"Going up into the hills on my mountain bike. Seven miles uphill and then the trail down where, if you screw up, you end up on the ground. The exhilaration you get from going so fast downhill makes up for all the work you did going uphill. The faster you go and the more rough it gets, the more exciting it is. I feel so relaxed after a good bike ride."

"I love to sit up until 3:00 a.m. talking to multiple friends on a bbs. We talk about everything and nothing. About 2:30, I check to see who's logged onto the whole system, and it says I've been logged on for 4 1/2 hours. Unbelievable."

"Personally, I experience an extreme high when I meditate. The relaxation involved, unlike any other method, releases such intense stress that I, in turn, become overjoyed. It is the overwhelming feeling of being content that delivers such a supreme high."

"Now it strikes me that I have had one long peak experience involving developmental and ethical challenges that shaped and changed how I see myself, life, and others. This takes the form of an emerging sense of journey which has developed through reflection, writing, and conversations, not in one pure realization. It seems like a communing of myself and a universal reality, a recognition of a truth that transcends each single experience."

"Working hard on something like studying for a really big test. Then going in to take it and being able to answer all the questions easily. That is a great feeling."

"Dreaming brings all parts of my life together. I seem to reach above my irrational, emotional level and think logically about my life as though I were looking at it from afar. I become different people in my dreams, which makes me relate more understandingly to people in my life. I write my dreams into stories and poems."

"While in the Navy, I was fortunate enough to attend the Basic Underwater Demolition School. One natural high was that of overcoming fear of extreme adversity. For example, in one exercise we were supposed to take our rafts over the surf. Every time we tried this, the surf slammed us back into the water. Thus, we were dragged underwater on the ocean floor until the current released us. After about 5-6 times, we began to enjoy it. We experienced feelings of great elation when it happened. When we finally made it past this surf, we felt regretful that it was over."

"My most wonderful high is being on the stage and performing for an audience who appreciates my acting and entertainment in general. It is one of the most powerful inducements to my brain, awakening, and heart. I feel I can fly after the play is over and the audience puts their hands together. It's a beautiful wonder."

"The birth of my best friend's daughter was an event I had waited 9 months for, but I still wasn't prepared. It was such an emotionally powerful experience that I lost all control."

"The best way I have found to get a natural high is to make an assessment of your own perceived limitations in any area and then to set out and purposely attempt to break through the barriers and limitations you have imagined. There is no bigger actual rush of the body, mind, and soul than to find you are able to surmount some obstacle that had become self-limiting."

"A trip to the park with my 4-year-old daughter. She brought me out of my cocaine addiction. Each day I spend watching her grow and expand is my recipe for a natural high. One of the best things to do in this world is to love a child. We should always remember the joy and love they bring us."

Altered States Of Consciousness

Natural Highs

Natural highs are intense, exhilarating experiences that offer healthy, life-affirming alternatives to substance-induced highs.

Everyone has the capacity to experience natural highs. They occur because the brain releases chemicals that reward success and sexuality, soothe us in times of stress, and energize us in times of physical danger or conflict. The potential for non-drug highs exists in all of us. Regular joggers may feel a "runner's high," involving euphoria and an altered state of consciousness that result from tapping into their natural endorphins, the brain's opiate-like chemicals. These feelings have been likened to a drug "high."

© 1994 Richard Roschke

Since heart-beating, mind-racing, natural highs are such desirable experiences, some people try to induce them artificially with alcohol and other psychoactive drugs. Why? These drugs, which affect many of the same brain chemicals that trigger natural highs, can create or intensify pleasant moods such as sociability and elation, or change undesirable ones, such as boredom and depression.

Many people's experiences with alcohol and drugs are initially positive. They get what they want: feeling different, relief from stress or pain, peer approval, challenge to authority. Regularly employing psychoactive substances as shortcuts to euphoria has consequences.

- Alcohol and other drugs can have side effects (hangovers, anxiety, depression, high blood pressure, health problems) which can last far longer than the desired effects; natural highs rarely do.

- The intensity of the substance-induced high diminishes over time (tolerance), requiring more and more of the substance to achieve a high or even to feel normal; natural highs often intensify over time.

- Because substances are quick, easy short-cuts, the tendency toward uncontrollable use can be overwhelming. Whereas non-drug highs can also become addicting (e.g., gambling, watching T.V., risk-taking, sexual activity), most are not.

- Drugs can short-circuit psychological and social maturation which includes learning how to solve problems, relate socially, and find pleasure and satisfaction naturally. Most natural highs enhance and encourage growth.

Workbook Exercise 1: Discuss why some people in our culture use tobacco, coffee, alcohol, and other drugs to get high rather than using natural means.

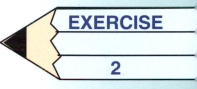

EXERCISE

1

_____

_____

_____

_____

_____

_____

_____

_____

_____

_____

_____

_____

Workbook Exercise 2: List several ways of feeling really good, altering your consciousness, or expanding your sense of self without drinking, smoking, or using other drugs in each of the following areas.

EXERCISE

2

Physical (e.g., a hard workout): _____

_____

_____

Intellectual (e.g., finishing a term paper on time): _____

_____

_____

Social (e.g., a great night of dancing): _____

_____

_____

Spiritual (e.g., looking at a clear, starry night): _____

_____

_____

Emotional (e.g., seeing a best friend after a long absence): _____

_____

_____

Workbook Exercise 3: Natural highs can be brief and fleeting (making a last-minute, winning score for your team), more enduring (learning to play a musical instrument you really love), or life-long (doing work you look forward to every day, watching your child grow). Describe what you personally do or could do to experience short-term, medium-term, and long-term natural highs.

1) Short-term, right now, in the next hour: _____

_____

_____

_____

_____

2) Medium-term, in the next semester, the coming year: _____

_____

_____

_____

_____

3) Long-term, something that will last your lifetime: _____

_____

_____

_____

_____

Group Exercise 1: With 2-3 other students, design a group activity which has a good chance of producing natural highs for participants. Consider including something new that breaks a routine, involves physical effort, or gets people emotionally involved. For example, a winter hike and picnic or singing in a group.

Group Exercise 2: Form 10 groups with each group responsible for discussing ways of achieving 1 of the following kinds of natural highs.

1) School-related natural high
2) Work-related natural high
3) Most frequently experienced natural high
4) Non-sexual, interpersonal natural high
5) Natural high that involves emotions
6) Athletic or physical natural high
7) Religious or spiritual natural high
8) Creative natural high
9) Intellectual or mental natural high
10) A natural peak experience; a personal best

Results can then be reported to the entire group.

Photograph by Laurie Lepore

_PI_ **Personal Inquiry:** Summarize a natural high you have had. Include what led up to it, the setting, the experience itself, and how you value it now.

A Matter Of Balance
Physical Health And Drugs

Taking responsibililty for one's physical well-being is the best way to control use of alcohol and other drugs.

> "Your health is your most important possession. Without it you'd be dead."
>
> Thomas Pynchon

One of the most important human survival traits is homeostasis, the body's natural drive to stay in equilibrium (balance). When we are hungry, thirsty, cold, or tired, we seek food, water, warmth, and sleep. When we are satisfying our needs, our body responds with a feeling of satisfaction or of pleasure. But when our needs are not being met, that drive to stay in balance can influence some individuals to use tobacco, alcohol, and other drugs. Excessive use of these substances can then destabilize their health even more, causing them to increase use just to stay normal.

By taking care of our physical needs before we become too hungry, too cold, too tired — too unbalanced — we begin to protect ourselves from becoming part of the more than 800,000 premature deaths each year in the United States as shown in the graph. Even if premature death does not occur, the quality of life is diminished when health is impaired.

If we go beyond just avoiding illness and try to maximize our health, we can feel better, look better, and gain greater satisfaction and fulfillment.

When we were young, we relied on others to satisfy our physical needs, prepare our meals, get us to bed, get us to the doctor, or make us take our medicine. As adults, that responsibility becomes our own. We have the choice to determine how well we live.

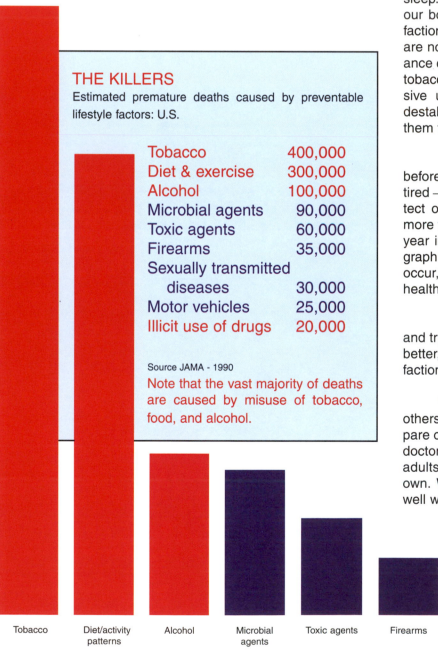

THE KILLERS

Estimated premature deaths caused by preventable lifestyle factors: U.S.

Tobacco	400,000
Diet & exercise	300,000
Alcohol	100,000
Microbial agents	90,000
Toxic agents	60,000
Firearms	35,000
Sexually transmitted diseases	30,000
Motor vehicles	25,000
Illicit use of drugs	20,000

Source JAMA - 1990

Note that the vast majority of deaths are caused by misuse of tobacco, food, and alcohol.

| Tobacco | Diet/activity patterns | Alcohol | Microbial agents | Toxic agents | Firearms | Sexually transmitted diseases | Motor vehicles | Illicit use of drugs |

> "Personally, when I have a craving or a strong thought to use cocaine, I pay attention to what areas of my life are not in sync. Am I too hungry? Am I bored? Because the only time that the compulsion comes up is when I'm not taking care of who I am."
>
> Recovering cocaine abuser

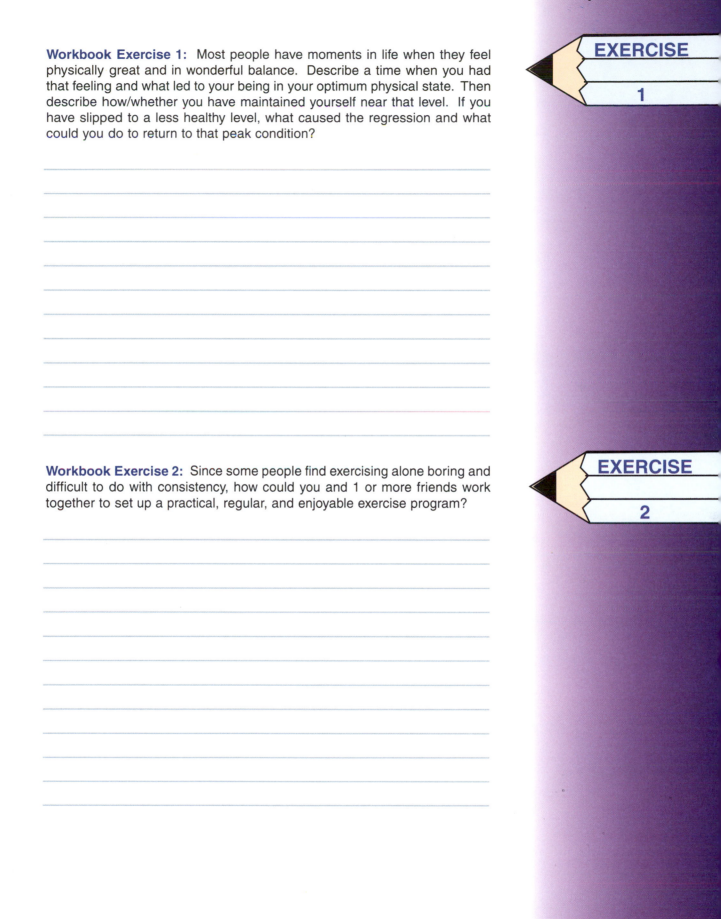

Workbook Exercise 1: Most people have moments in life when they feel physically great and in wonderful balance. Describe a time when you had that feeling and what led to your being in your optimum physical state. Then describe how/whether you have maintained yourself near that level. If you have slipped to a less healthy level, what caused the regression and what could you do to return to that peak condition?

EXERCISE

1

Workbook Exercise 2: Since some people find exercising alone boring and difficult to do with consistency, how could you and 1 or more friends work together to set up a practical, regular, and enjoyable exercise program?

EXERCISE

2

EXERCISE 3

Workbook Exercise 3: To decide whether you wish to change the way you care for yourself, it helps to assess your state of health. Use the following survey to reflect on your own health. The survey can also be used to assess the effects of any changes you decide to make. **Bring an anonymous copy of your assessment to class for the group exercise.**

Overall physical health:
_____ Male or female
_____ Height
_____ Weight
_____ Resting heart rate
_____ Blood pressure (optional)
_____ Are you currently ill?
_____ How many colds or sore throats do you get in a year?
_____ Estimate of your overall physical health (circle one):
      excellent   good   average   fair   poor

Sleep:
_____ Do you feel rested right now?
_____ How many hours did you sleep last night?
_____ Do you feel you need a nap during most days?
_____ Do you often doze off during the day?
_____ Do you take anything to help you sleep?
_____ Do you take anything to get you going?
_____ Do you take anything to stay awake?

Diet:
_____ How many meals did you eat yesterday?
_____ How many meals were "fast food?"
_____ Do you feel you ate too much, too little, or just right yesterday (circle one)?
_____ Are you currently on a diet?
_____ How many glasses of water did you drink in the last 24 hours?
_____ How many 12-oz. sugared soft drinks did you have?
_____ How many caffeinated drinks did you have?
_____ How many candy bars, pastries, or sweet desserts did you have?
What food makes up the bulk of your diet? Rank from 1(most) to 6(least).
    _____ Fruits and vegetables
    _____ Carbohydrates (e.g., whole grains, breads, pasta, beans, potatoes)
    _____ Beef, pork, lamb
    _____ Cheese, milk, eggs
    _____ Chicken or fish
    _____ Candy, snack foods, desserts

Exercise:
_____ How many minutes did you exercise yesterday?
_____ How often did you exercise last week?
_____ Do you prefer aerobic or strength exercises? (circle one)
_____ Do you walk/cycle on a regular basis? (circle one)
_____ Do you jog/run on a regular basis? (circle one)
_____ Do you play any sports?
_____ Are you easily winded?
_____ Do you feel you have sufficient physical strength for daily chores?
_____ Are you currently suffering pain from exercise?
_____ Give an overall estimate of your fitness (circle one):
      excellent   good   average   fair   poor

People who take psychoactive drugs often do so for their mental effects. Most drugs also cause physical effects. With increased use, the mental and physical effects occur at different rates, so as use increases, the amount needed to get high mentally can cause serious problems physically (and mentally).

Substance	Desired Mental (or Physical) Effects	Physical (or Mental) Side Effects from Heavy Use
Coffee	To wake up, alertness	Acid stomach, irritability, rapid heart beat
Tobacco	Stimulation, relaxation	Smoker's cough, bronchitis, irritability, cancer
Alcohol	Lowered inhibitions, muscular relaxation	Slowed reflexes, confusion, blackouts, liver damage
Cocaine	Intense stimulation	High blood pressure, mania, cardiac problems, paranoia

DOONESBURY

by Garry Trudeau

GROUP EXERCISE

Group Exercise 1: Collect and average the results of the health assessments completed in Workbook Exercise 3. Share the averages with the entire class. Then in small groups, discuss the results (e.g., Is there anything to be learned from the results? Are there any surprises? How could people use this information?)

Group Exercise 2: In small groups, discuss the ways you might be affected physically by the drug use of others (e.g., second-hand smoke, heavy drinking and then driving a car). Discuss ways to counter those effects.

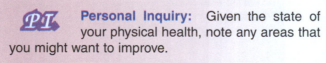

Personal Inquiry: Given the state of your physical health, note any areas that you might want to improve.

Putting It All Together
Developing A Totally Healthy Lifestyle

This chapter examines wellness, a philosophy of living that strives
to optimize intellectual, emotional, spiritual, social,
and physical health.

In the previous chapter, we discussed the body's drive to stay in balance physically. That drive also extends to other areas of our lives. Many counselors say that if we want to reach our optimum state of health, we need also to develop mentally, emotionally, spiritually and socially. This optimum state of health is called wellness. The concept is that all these facets of personality and physical being affect each other and that if you neglect one part, you diminish the others.

Wellness also provides an excellent alternative to alcohol and other drug use since it can give the feeling of well-being and intense satisfaction that some seek through drugs. Wellness is not easy. It requires knowledge, dedication, and persistence. Though very few, if any, achieve perfection in life, everyone can progress towards an ideal balance. As the philosopher John Locke said 300 years ago, "A sound mind in a sound body is a short but full description of a happy state in this world." There are many paths one can take towards an ideal balance.

Intellectual: "I have a full schedule and work part-time, but I still do a half-hour of exploratory reading each week and attend at least 1 lecture or cultural event per month. This is my quality time."

Marc - college senior

Emotional:
"If I'm down, I make sure I talk to somebody. I don't ignore those feelings. When someone says, 'You shouldn't feel like that,' I say, 'I feel what I feel,' but I can then direct those feelings in a positive way."

Tiffany - college junior

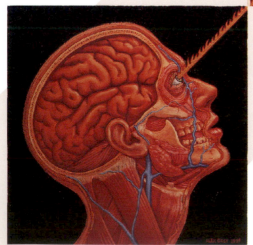

Body, Mind, Spirit, 1985 by ALEX GREY

Spiritual: "Being away from my home, I felt like I was out of place. I started thinking about what I believe in. I went to a campus forum on religion and then attended a class on meditation and one on spirituality; I went to different campus church meetings; I volunteered for 'Habitat for Humanity' to better understand these ideas. I feel that when I know what I believe in, I will know where I'm going."

John - college senior

Social: "In high school, I always admired, or should I say envied, those that could get up and speak, or were able to stand up for themselves, or who made friends easily. So I became involved in student government to overcome my fears. I tell you it's just amazing who you meet and what you get to talk about."

Kirsten - college sophomore

Workbook Exercise 1: Take a quick inventory of a few facets of your personality to better understand your strengths and weaknesses. Briefly explore 1 question from each set.

Intellectual:
1) What has challenged your mind recently?
2) Do you look for new intellectual challenges?
3) How do you care for and feed your mind?

Question # _____ Discussion: _____

_____

_____

_____

_____

Emotional:
1) What's the most frequent emotion you felt last month?
2) Do you seek out or avoid strong emotions?
3) Which kind of emotion do you value the most?

Question # _____ Discussion: _____

_____

_____

_____

_____

Spiritual or Inner Life (e.g., religious worship of God or a "higher power," a value or idea, nature, world peace, feeling awe at the universe):
1) What calms you when things become tough?
2) What values are most important to you?
3) How do you nourish your spiritual or inner life?

Question # _____ Discussion: _____

_____

_____

_____

_____

Social:
1) How many strangers have you interacted with in the last 48 hours? How pleasant was the interaction?
2) Characterize your relationship with classmates or co-workers (friendly, courteous, strained, etc.).
3) Are you emotionally available to family or friends for support; to listen when they need a friendly ear?

Question # _____ Discussion: _____

_____

_____

_____

_____

EXERCISE 2

Workbook Exercise 2: Assess your state of balance. Indicate how satisfied you are currently with your progress in the 5 areas of wellness by drawing a solid line across each bar .

	Physical	Intellectual	Emotional	Spiritual	Social

Very content

Content

Neutral

Concerned

Very dissatisfied

Now draw a dotted line across each bar to indicate where you would like to be. In the space below, write up a plan you could use to get where you want to be in 2 of the 5 areas.

Example: Emotional - At least once a week I will talk to a friend about my disappointments. Spiritual - I will give myself at least 5 quiet minutes in the morning to listen to my "inner voice."

1) Area: _____ Plan: _____

_____

_____

_____

_____

_____

_____

_____

_____

_____

2) Area: _____ Plan: _____

_____

_____

_____

_____

_____

_____

_____

_____

_____

Group Exercise 1: Divide the class into 5 groups and then have each group report on local resources or facilities (a foreign language club, a regular lecture series, etc.) that help individuals to develop physically, intellectually, emotionally, spiritually, and socially.

Group Exercise 2: Divide into small groups. Have each group discuss which physical, intellectual, emotional, spiritual, and social qualities they think would make an ideal 21-year-old man and an ideal 21-year-old woman. Then discuss the ideals with the rest of the class.

PI **Personal Inquiry:** Discuss which aspects of your wellness (physical, intellectual, emotional, spiritual, or social) are most responsible for your decision not to use or overuse psychoactive substances.

CHAPTER 9

Your Mirror Image

Maintaining Self-Respect

By affirming and developing a positive image of ourselves, we are aided in making positive life choices, including ones about drinking and drug use.

> **"** "Self-love, my liege, is not so vile a sin as self-neglecting."
>
> Shakespeare, *King Henry V*

With a belief in our intrinsic self-worth, we are better able to take responsibility for our actions, to recognize our achievements, and to go forward with our lives. If we let criticisms from others or from our own inner voice affect us too much, the challenge then is to counter these criticisms, especially our own, with positive thoughts and actions.

Low self-esteem is thought to be one of the factors that predisposes people to abuse substances. It can result from negative experiences — a trauma in early childhood (injury or sexual abuse), from a non-nurturing childhood, excessive criticism by teachers or parents, ridicule from peers, or a negative attitude. This might include unfavorable perceptions of one's own physical and mental attributes or insecurity about one's appearance, class, or ethnic origins. A negative attitude towards oneself can result in many kinds of unhealthy emotions and behaviors, including looking to alcohol or other drugs to block out the voices of criticism and doubt.

FYI Thought Stopping

For those times when you are really down on yourself and you know your self-critical thoughts are not being constructive, practice the art of thought stopping. Try saying to yourself mentally, "Stop it!" "That's enough!" Or if it's difficult to stop a thought with another thought, distract yourself by taking a deep breath, exercising, or calling a friend.

A healthy sense of self-worth is a first line of defense against drug abuse. Self-worth is a quality that is developed over time. Replace a negative thought with a positive, self-affirming one, and you make a contribution to your self-esteem.

Exercises Chapter 9

Workbook Exercise 1:   Using this informal survey, assess the condition of your self-respect by indicating 1, 2, or 3 after each of the following.

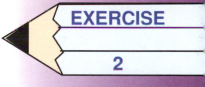

Positives:	Rarely 1	Sometimes 2	Often 3
1) I am proud of my accomplishments.			
2) I welcome success.			
3) I accept my mistakes and work towards fixing them.			
4) I feel people will gain from friendship with me.			
5) I accept the way I look.			
6) I feel I can choose my future rather than react to it.			
7) I trust myself and try to protect myself.			
8) I take responsibility for my actions no matter what.			
9) I like myself.			

Negatives:	Rarely 3	Sometimes 2	Often 1
1) I think that most people I meet won't like me.			
2) I isolate myself.			
3) I don't listen to others.			
4) I dislike how I look.			
5) I overreact to criticism.			
6) I have trouble working persistently for a goal.			
7) I lose myself in obsessive activities such as studying, working, food, alcohol, or even drugs.			
8) I often try to please others rather than myself.			
9) I find it difficult to face up to my mistakes.			

(If your score is well over 36, you probably have a healthy self-respect. If it is well under 36, you probably could do some work to help you feel better about yourself.)

Workbook Exercise 2: Briefly describe the qualities in yourself that you could draw on to keep from beginning or progressing to an unhealthy relationship with alcohol and other drugs.

_____

_____

_____

_____

_____

_____

EXERCISE

3

Workbook Exercise 3: Briefly describe 3 good habits or traits you have.

1) _____
   _____

2) _____
   _____

3) _____
   _____

Describe your greatest accomplishment. _____
_____

What is the greatest compliment you have ever received? _____
_____

What is the greatest compliment you have ever given someone? _____
_____

List 3 positive words others would use to describe you.

1) _____ 2) _____ 3) _____

What makes you feel good about yourself? _____
_____
_____
_____

When you are really feeling good about yourself, how do you let others know?
What do you say? What do you wear? How do you look?

_____
_____
_____
_____
_____
_____
_____
_____

Group Exercise 1: Form pairs and interview each other about personal strengths and achievements. Think of yourself as the press agent or advocate for your partner. Then introduce your partner to groups of 6-8 in the most favorable light based on what the person has told you about his/her strengths or achievements.

Group Exercise 2: In small groups, explore the following questions: How do people with positive self-images get them? How do they keep developing them? How can a positive self-image be lost? Regained? What is the difference between bragging and projecting a positive self-image?

> **❝** "One thing my father told me when I was young that kept me from beating myself up when I made a mistake was, `Understand why it happened, accept that you are human and can make mistakes, forgive yourself, get rid of the guilt (but don't condone the mistake), and most important, don't do it again.'"
>
> College instructor

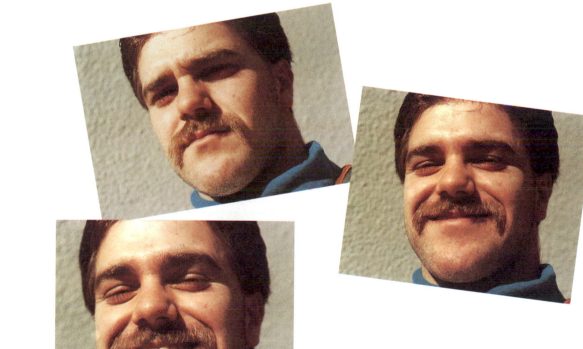

𝒫ℐ **Personal Inquiry:** If you were to die tomorrow what would your epitaph be? If you were to die at the age of 70, what do you hope your epitaph would be?

Driving The Inner-State
Making Personal Changes

This chapter offers you the opportunity to reflect on Chapters 1-9, to summarize personal changes that you wrote about or discussed, and to practice techniques you can use to undertake those changes.

Change is doing it, not just hoping it will get done, or waiting for someone else to do it, or even saying you'll try. But change is hard, and the more ingrained the habit and the older you become, the more difficult it becomes to move in a different direction.

Changing yourself is hard work, but not as hard as having to change someone else in order to be happy. Luckily, there is an excitement generated by trying and expecting success that often gets the whole process started. Each success makes each new attempt easier to complete.

To change, you may have to overcome some of the following:

- Force of habit;
- Fear of the discomfort changing would cause;
- Others' expectations that you will stay the same;
- The wish that something good will happen with no effort on your part;
- Lack of confidence that you can change;
- Distraction.

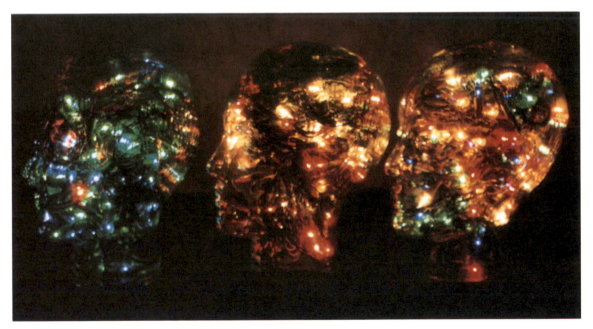

❝ "I used to think, 'Why can't people judge me by my intentions, not by what I do?' Later on in life I realized that there's a shortage of mind readers."

23-year-old MIT graduate

FYI You are ready to make changes when

- Physical, emotional or financial costs of not acting are too great to bear.
- Situations (place, people, job) change, and old behavior patterns no longer work.
- The rewards of changing outweigh the comfort of not changing.
- Other people who have successfully solved difficulties or answered challenges serve as models.
- People around you reassure you, instill confidence, and support your efforts to change.

FYI Part of making changes is solving a series of problems. Practicing one's ability to solve individual problems can be a valuable asset for making overall changes. The acronym PILLAR can be used to remember 6 steps to solving a problem.

- **Problem:** Put the problem in writing so that you can focus on it.
- **Intuition:** Trust your intuition. What do you feel in your gut that you need to do?
- **List alternatives:** Brainstorm. Get input from those around you. Consider as many options as possible.
- **List pros and cons.** Anticipate the consequences of various actions.
- **Action plan:** Choose and devise a plan. List specific actions in the order they need to be done. Carry out the plan.
- **Reevaluate:** A successful outcome may require several attempts. Persevere.

Workbook Exercise 1: Pick a specific problem that you wish to solve which relates to 1 of the areas you wrote about in any of the previous chapters. Then devise a plan of action using the above steps.

EXERCISE

1

1) Area of change: _____

_____

2) What does your intuition tell you to do? _____

_____

_____

_____

3) List alternative courses of action:

Alt. 1: _____

Alt. 2: _____

4) List pros and cons:

	Pros	Cons
Alt. 1:		
Alt. 2:		

5) Action plan: _____

1st action: _____

_____ by (date) _____

2nd action: _____

_____ by (date) _____

3rd action: _____

_____ by (date) _____

EXERCISE 2

Workbook Exercise 2: Complete the following:

1) Realistically, an area (not just a problem) that I could begin to work on now is

2) Benefits I foresee from working on this include

3) Three skills I have that would help me change in this area are

   a)

   b)

   c)

4) Three things that might hinder me in changing are

   a)

   b)

   c)

5) Acknowledging that change can be difficult, in order to change I am willing to give up

6) Once I actually begin, the excuses I have to avoid for not completing the change are

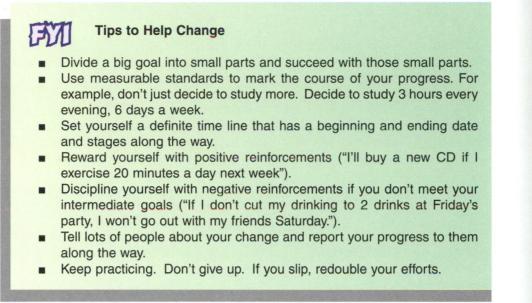
Group Exercise 1: Divide into 5 groups, depending on whether you want to focus primarily on physical, social, spiritual, intellectual, or emotional change. Then have each group discuss how they could provide mutual support for each other's change projects (e.g., study group, support group, tutoring).

Group Exercise 2: Divide into small groups and have each person relate a story about how he or she was able to change some behavior. Discuss the specific steps that were taken.

Personal Inquiry: Make a contract with yourself to change some area of your life that you wish to strengthen.

PERSONAL CHANGE CONTRACT

I, _____ (*your name*), on _____ (*today's date*), agree to change, strengthen, or begin to do the following:

_____

_____ I will share this commitment with

_____

(*name of person(s)* and by _____ (*future date*), I will report back to the above person(s) about the outcome of this agreement and my ideas and feelings about my experiences.

Signed _____

PART II: ENVIRONMENTAL PRESSURES TO USE

CHAPTERS 11-20 OVERVIEW

Some elements of our culture promote alcohol and other drug use as a shortcut — a softer, easier, and quicker way to enjoy ourselves, to socialize, to cure boredom, to assert independence, or to be accepted as an adult. There are also protective influences in our communities, culture, and environment that can help us moderate or resist use.

Chapters 11-20 emphasize how those around us, our communities, and more generally, our culture can exert powerful influences on us, either to use, to resist use, or to moderate use of psychoactive substances. These chapters help develop skills in coping with environmental influences in order to reduce any harmful potential.

Chapter 11 explores how an individual perceives a "normal" or "usual" level of use by others and how that perception can influence his or her decision to use. **Chapter 12** examines additional protective factors, namely the standards for use of psychoactive substances that exist in various cultures and communities. **Chapter 13** looks at the influences from the media that encourage use,

and **Chapter 14** examines the pressures tobacco companies exert to buy their products while ignoring the heavily addicting properties of nicotine. **Chapter 15** further explores environmental influences on choices to abstain or use by focusing on the issues surrounding psychoactive substances in rites of passages and conceptions of adult behavior.

The next 4 chapters present techniques and strategies for dealing with the consequences of using psychoactive substances. **Chapter 16** shows how strong social skills help avoid reliance on alcohol and drugs as an aid in relationships or as a focus for social occasions. **Chapter 17** takes up topics dealing with the interaction of alcohol and other drugs and sexual activity. **Chapter 18** introduces ways of protecting oneself against anger and violence, especially when related to psychoactive drugs, and **Chapter 19** suggests ways of reducing the risks and harm associated with alcohol use. **Chapter 20** then offers the opportunity to review the previous chapters and to consider making positive changes in one's environment.

Doesn't Everyone?

Normative Assessment

The mistaken perception that most people abuse alcohol and other drugs can persuade someone to use or abuse. Misperceptions can be corrected by becoming aware of the actual levels of use.

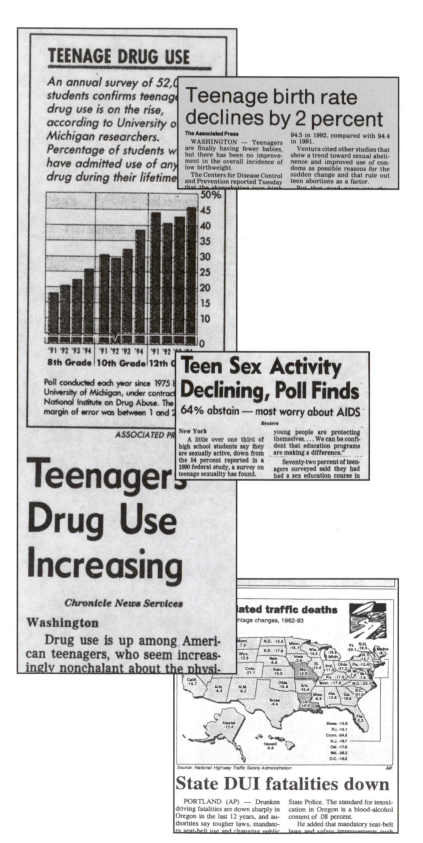

There are those who try to teach us to avoid alcohol and other drugs with a "Just say NO" philosophy. But "Just say NO" is only a partial solution to a complex problem. The reasons people use or abuse are often immune to relying only on this approach.

Others try to teach us to resist alcohol or drugs by using scare tactics: e.g., negative health effects, celebrity overdoses, or threats of arrest. Warnings or scare tactics can backfire if people feel that dire consequences are not as prevalent as claimed, don't apply to them, or exaggerate the bad effects. As a result, scare tactics lead some people to doubt any prevention message.

On the other hand, the desire to use and even abuse can be encouraged by our perception or misperception of society's and especially our peers' behavior. For example, if someone thinks that the norm is to drink a 6-pack in 1 sitting or to smoke a pack of cigarettes a day, that can encourage him or her to do the same whether or not it is true.

Most people perceive the level of use of alcohol and other drugs to be much higher than it actually is.

For this reason, it is helpful to know the facts about the actual levels of consumption when deciding whether or how much to use.

It can also be helpful to your community to make that knowledge known to aid others in making informed decisions. In any community information campaign, it is worth keeping in mind that there are less effective and more effective ways to present information. For example, the newspapers could publicize the fact that 16% of students on campus caused physical harm to themselves or others as a consequence of drinking. On the other hand, they could emphasize the fact that 84% did **not** cause any harm or that 98% of students **never were arrested** on a DUI (driving under the influence) charge.

Normative Assessment Survey (Anonymous)

Taking and then analyzing the results of this **anonymous** survey will give you a better idea of the prevalence of drugs and drinking, other substance use patterns, and other behavior in your group. It will also help compare expectations to reality. When finished, turn the surveys over to a committee to tabulate the results.

Circle the appropriate response or fill in the blank. (One drink is defined as a 12-oz. beer, a 5-oz. glass of wine, a 1 1/2-oz. shot of liquor by itself or with a mixer.)

1) Which statement best represents your attitude?
   A. Drinking is never a good thing to do.
   B. Drinking is all right, but a person should never get "smashed."
   C. An occasional "drunk" is okay as long as it doesn't interfere with responsibilities.
   D. An occasional "drunk" is okay even if it does interfere with responsibilities.
   E. A frequent "drunk" is okay if that's what somebody wants to do.

2) Which of the above statements best represents the unspoken attitude on your campus?
   A   B   C   D   E

3) How frequently do you drink?
   A. Don't drink   B. 1 - 2X per year   C. 1 - 2X per month
   D. 1X per week   E. 2 - 3X per week   F. More than 3X per week

4) The last time you drank, how many drinks did you have?
   A. 0   B. 1 - 2   C. 3 - 5   D. 6 - 9   E. 10 or more

5) Normally, when you party, how many drinks do you have on the average?
   A. 0   B. 1 - 2   C. 3 - 5   D. 6 - 9   E. 10 or more

6) What percentage of college students drinks at least once a week?
   A. 20%   B. 30%   C. 45%   D. 60%   E. 75%

7) Within the last academic year, how many times, if any, did the following occur as a consequence of your use of alcohol? This is meant to check the frequency of negative consequences. If it didn't occur, write N.
   ___ Physically injured another   ___ Physically injured yourself
   ___ Got into a fight   ___ Damaged property
   ___ Had an unwanted sexual experience   ___ Damaged relationship
   ___ Had a memory loss   ___ Arrested for DUI
   ___ Felt depressed   ___ Vomited or became ill
   ___ Got drunk   ___ Used alcohol & drugs together
   ___ Performed poorly on job or at school ___ Missed exam at school or deadline
   ___ Got into an argument

8) What percentage of the college population do you think became ill or vomited 4 or more times per year due to drinking?
   A. 1 - 5%   B. 6 - 10%   C. 11 - 20%   D. 21 - 40%   E. 41% or more

9) What percentage of students do you think used marijuana in the last month?
   A. 1 - 3%   B. 4 - 9%   C. 10 - 14%   D. 15 - 17%   E. 18 - 26%

10) Which of the following do you use?
    A. Cigarettes   B. Smokeless tobacco   C. A & B   D. Neither   E. Cigar or pipe

11) If you use tobacco, how frequently do you smoke or chew?
   A. Once a month   B. 2 - 4X per month   C. 1 - 2 X per week   D. Every day

12) What percentage of the **U.S.** population do you think uses tobacco on a daily basis?
   A. 1 - 5%   B. 6 - 10%   C. 11 - 20%   D. 21 - 30%   E. 31 - 40%

13) What percentage of the **college** population do you think uses tobacco on a daily basis?
   A. 5%   B. 15%   C. 25%   D. 35%   E. 45%

14) What percentage of people who smoke do you think want to quit?
   A. 60%   B. 70%   C. 80%   D. 90%   E. 100%

15) What percentage of college students do you think has **never** smoked marijuana?
   A. 20 - 29%   B. 30 - 49%   C. 50 - 64%   D. 65 - 79%   E. 80 - 100%

16) What proportion of the college population do you think has **never** used amphetamines?
   A. Under 50% B. 60%   C. 70%   D. 80%   E. 90%

17) What percentage of the college population thinks that they have a problem with alcohol
   or other drugs?
   A. 0 - 5%   B. 10 - 15%   C. 20 - 25%   D. 30 - 35%   E. 40 - 45%

18) What percentage of college students do you think would prefer a drug-free campus environment?
   A. Under 50% B. 50 - 60%   C. 61 - 70%   D. 71 - 80%   E. 81 - 90%

19) What percentage of college students do you think would prefer an alcohol-free campus
   environment?
   A. 20 - 25%   B. 30 - 35%   C. 40 - 45%   D. 50 - 55%   E. 60 - 65%

20) How many hours of TV do you watch per week?
   A. None   B. 1 - 2   C. 3 - 5   D. 6 - 8   E. 9 or more

21) How many hours do you exercise per week?
   A. 0   B. 1   C. 2 - 4   D. 5 - 7   E. 8 or more

22) Does your college have an alcohol and drug abuse prevention program?
   A. Yes   B. No   C. Don't know

23) How many partners did you have sex with last year?
   A. 0   B. 1   C. 2   D. 3 - 4   E. 5 or more

24) How many partners do you think college students have sex with in 1 year?
   A. 0   B. 1   C. 2   D. 3 - 4   E. 5 or more

The answers to questions 6, 8, 9, 13, 14, 15, 16, 17, 18, 19 can be found on page 146.

These questions were adapted from a CORE survey developed by Southern Illinois University.
For more information about the survey, contact the CORE Institute, Student Health Programs,
Southern Illinois University at Carbondale, Carbondale, Illinois 62901.

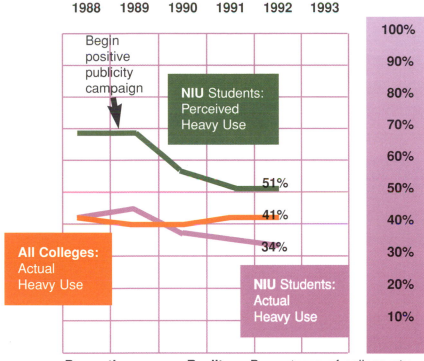

1988   1989   1990   1991   1992   1993

Begin positive publicity campaign

NIU Students: Perceived Heavy Use

51%

41%

34%

All Colleges: Actual Heavy Use

NIU Students: Actual Heavy Use

100%
90%
80%
70%
60%
50%
40%
30%
20%
10%

Perception versus Reality -- Percentages of college students who are heavy drinkers (e.g., those who have had 5 or more drinks at 1 sitting at least once every 2 weeks).

FYI In 1988, students at Northern Illinois University thought that 70% of the students were heavy drinkers whereas the real numbers were closer to the national average of 43%. The following year, the University started publicizing the real numbers. When the students saw them, they reduced their level of heavy drinking by almost 25% , well below the national average. Their perception of the amount of heavy use also dropped dramatically. **When many students realized that not everyone was a heavy drinker, it took much of the pressure off of them to drink.**

Group Exercise: Evaluate the tabulated responses from the Normative Assessment Survey and discuss the following topics:

1) Which results on questions 6, 8, 9, 12-19, 24 about **perception** surprised you because they were either higher or lower than expected?
2) Which results on questions 1, 3, 4, 5, 7, 10, 11, 20, 21, 22, 23 about your group's **actual use** surprised you? Why?
3) Did you think the non-use of alcohol would be higher or lower than it actually was?
4) How does your class compare in the heavy drinking category to the national average shown in the graph?
5) Account for any divergence between your class results and the national averages shown on this page and on p. 146.

GROUP EXERCISE

PI   Personal Inquiry: Write about something you have done that you didn't feel good about but went ahead and did anyway because you thought most people were doing it (e.g., heavy drinking, sex, etc.).

Report Says More College Women Binge Drinking

Statistics show sharp increase — from 10% in 1977 to 35% today

Associated Press

Washington

College campuses are awash in alcohol, with white men the biggest drinkers but a quickly increasing number of women now getting drunk as well, a commission of academic and civic leaders said yesterday.

"Binge drinking on our cam

■ In 90 percent of all campus rapes, the assailant, the victim or both had been drinking.

■ Sixty percent of college women who acquire sexually transmitted diseases, including herpes and AIDS, were drunk at the time of infection.

It's A Way Of Life
Protective Traditions In Cultures And Communities

Because psychoactive substances are used in many cultures and communities, knowing their traditions and standards of responsible use and safe practices can help reduce harmful effects.

© 1995 Eric Johnson

Although tobacco is smoked in the Native American pipe ceremony, it is not inhaled. The smoke from the pipe bowl is the breath from the people carrying their prayers to the Creator.

Recognizing the mind-altering properties of psychoactive substances, various cultures use them as a sacrament in religious ceremonies; for convivial and recreational purposes; as food and beverages; as medicines or anesthetics; and in many other ways. On the other hand, these substances can be destructive and destabilize a family, community, or culture. Therefore, use is often controlled by cultural norms and limitations based on factors such as age, sex, profession, and class.

Controlled access can be seen as a culture's compromise, its endeavor to simultaneously make available and restrict these substances. All or nothing philosophies often backfire. Strenuous attempts to prohibit alcohol and other drugs can make them more desirable and promote more risky activities than those prohibited. On the other hand, legalization of drugs can lead to excessive use as seen by the rates of alcohol- and tobacco-related diseases and social problems in the U.S.

Examples of protective mechanisms used by a culture to regulate use are laws, taxes, social pressure, and taboos. Some of the protective mechanisms used to reduce harm include initiation rituals, education, sensible customs, and acceptable norms.

FYI Different cultures use different practices to control use of alcohol or tobacco and, hopefully, promote moderate use and reduce harm. In Italy, wine is served with food and is given, watered down, to children at family meals. (Unfortunately, statistics have shown a rising rate of alcoholism in Italy -- 16% in 1993.) In most Mormon, Adventist, and Muslim households in the U.S., alcohol is not served because it is prohibited by their religions. Native American tribes use tobacco (some use peyote) in a sacramental context and discourage regular use.

Workbook Exercise 1: By checking a __ or u __ , indicate what drugs are considered **a**cceptable or **u**nacceptable by your family, campus, neighborhood, and culture.

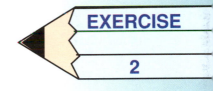

EXERCISE

1

Substance:	Family	Campus	Neighborhood	Culture
Tea/coffee	a __ u __	a __ u __	a __ u __	a __ u __
Alcohol	a __ u __	a __ u __	a __ u __	a __ u __
Cigarettes	a __ u __	a __ u __	a __ u __	a __ u __
Marijuana	a __ u __	a __ u __	a __ u __	a __ u __
Cocaine	a __ u __	a __ u __	a __ u __	a __ u __
Amphetamine	a __ u __	a __ u __	a __ u __	a __ u __
LSD	a __ u __	a __ u __	a __ u __	a __ u __
Others (specify)				
_____	a __ u __	a __ u __	a __ u __	a __ u __
_____	a __ u __	a __ u __	a __ u __	a __ u __
_____	a __ u __	a __ u __	a __ u __	a __ u __

Workbook Exercise 2: Name a culture, religion, or ethnic group you are familiar with and a psychoactive substance which is considered acceptable by that culture. Then describe several protective measures with which the culture encourages acceptable use and discourages abuse. For example, some Jewish families serve grape juice to children instead of wine at Passover.

EXERCISE

2

Culture/ethnic group: _____   Substance: _____

Protective Measures:

1) _____
_____
_____
_____
_____
_____

2) _____
_____
_____
_____
_____
_____

3) _____
_____
_____
_____
_____
_____

Workbook Exercise 3: Write about whether cultures that introduce alcohol to children/adolescents, such as including it with meals, watering it down, using it with rituals and holidays, are preparing young people to be responsible drinkers or setting them up for alcohol-related problems in later life.

Workbook Exercise 4: Because alcohol and other drugs are part of the campus community, each campus has developed rules, standards, and practices, both official and unofficial, regarding use. Part of the campus "cultural" response has been to provide education, create support systems, formulate policy, enforce laws and regulations, and provide counseling and referral services.

With respect to alcohol and other drug use and dating and sexual practices, write about how campus traditions and practices conflict with or continue the culture you were in before you came to college.

1) Alcohol and other drug use:

2) Dating and sexual practices:

Group Exercise 1: In the '60's, many people subscribed to a pro-drug and free-love culture that started with good intentions but eventually generated numerous problems, including the cocaine and AIDS epidemics. Based on the diverse family and cultural resources available in your class, formulate your own campus customs, protective strategies, traditions regarding alcohol and other drug use, dating, and sexual practices which will hopefully avoid the mistakes of previous generations.

FYI Alcohol and Other Drugs Use (1993) by Ethnic Groups and by Sex (twelve years old and up)
National Household Survey on Drug Abuse - National Institute on Drug Abuse

	Total Population	Caucasian	African-Americans	Hispanic-Americans	Male	Female
Totals	207 mil.	158 mil	23 mil.	18 mil.	99 mil.	108 mil.
Substance	**Percentages who used in last 30 days**					
Alcohol						
Casual use	49.6%	52.7%	37.6%	45.6%	57.4%	42.5%
* Heavy use	5.3%	5.7%	4.3%	5.2%	9.5%	1.5%
Cigarettes	23.4%	24.7%	21.2%	22.4%	26.2%	22.3%
Any illicit						
drug	5.6%	5.5%	6.8%	6.2%	7.4%	4.1%
Marijuana	4.3%	4.2%	5.6%	4.7%	6.0%	2.8%
Cocaine	0.6%	0.5%	1.3%	1.1%	0.9%	0.4%

* *Heavy use means 5 or more drinks in a row at least once every 2 weeks.*

Group Exercise 2: To what extent do the figures in the above chart correspond to general opinions about the extent of use by the various gender and ethnic groups?

PI Based on your personal and cultural values, what traditions would you pass on to your children regarding alcohol and other drug use?

The Medium Is The Message

Thinking Critically About The Media

This chapter will help you critically evaluate media messages that make alcohol and drug use or abuse look attractive.

40,000 Commercials

We are all bombarded by the media which offer us endless entertainment and consumer products. It's easy to dismiss the extent of the influence of advertising, television shows, films, and music, but the average American is exposed to 40,000 commercials, 912 hours of television, dozens of feature-length films, and thousands of songs per year. We may think we are immune to these messages, but almost everyone is influenced by some aspect of the media.

912 Hours Of TV

The most common message in the 90's is "There is a quicker, easier way to do anything in life, so why deny yourself?" Advertisements, television programs, films, and songs present products and represent behaviors as shortcuts to love, health, happiness, and pleasure. Life's problems appear to be easily solved in a half-hour sitcom, a 1-hour drama, or, if it's really complicated, a 6-hour mini-series.

Even though we know how illogical, manipulative, and untrue to life some media messages can be, there must be some reason advertisers continue to spend billions of dollars annually to influence us.

Workbook Exercise 1: Pick a current TV show or movie. Describe how it portrays the following:

T.V. show or movie: _____

1) Current clothing or hairstyles: _____

_____

_____

_____

2) Desirable/undesirable personality traits: _____

_____

_____

_____

3) Typical conflicts and ways they are resolved: _____

_____

_____

_____

4) Stated or implied norms, standards, or values: _____

_____

_____

_____

FYI There are a number of accurate portrayals of substance use and abuse in motion pictures that are worth viewing: *Barfly, Bird, Drug Store Cowboy, The Doors, Lady Sings the Blues, The Rose, Sid and Nancy, A Star is Born, The Days of Wine and Roses, Clean and Sober, New Jack City, I'm Dancing as Fast as I Can, Postcards from the Edge,* and *Coal Miner's Daughter.*

Workbook Exercise 2: Ads are carefully constructed to create a halo around a product or to make people identify with and desire it. Find a print ad for either alcohol, tobacco, or other consumer products and answer the following questions about them:

Ad 1: Product: _____

Summary of ad: _____

_____

_____

_____

Implied or stated advantages of product: _____

_____

_____

_____

Emotion or mood conveyed: _____

_____

Contribution of setting, models, background: _____

_____

_____

_____

JASON MOSS

Workbook Exercise 3: For each of the products below, describe what an advertiser would need to include in the advertisement in order to influence you to buy that product:

Jeans: _____

_____

_____

Perfume or cologne: _____

_____

_____

Cold medicines: _____

_____

_____

Beer (if you drink; if you don't, coffee, soft drink, or other favorite beverage): _____

_____

_____

Cigarettes or smokeless tobacco (if you use; if not, candy or snack food): _____

_____

FYI **ADVERTISING TECHNIQUES**

1) Sex Appeal ("Make things happen." -- Ambassador whiskey ad)
2) Have fun (show people playing softball and drinking Miller's Beer)
3) Advance you into manhood or womanhood (The Marlboro Man)
4) Comparison ("Our brand has 50% more pain relievers.")
5) Snob appeal ("Do you have any Grey Poupon Mustard?")
6) Join the crowd ("The most popular car in America")
7) Symbol (Joe Camel)
8) Personal testimony ("I'm amazed, it does work better.")
9) Mockery or put down ("You've got morning breath. You need Scope.")
10) Be healthy ("Flatten your stomach with Nordic Trac.")
11) Take control of your life ("Just do it!" -- Nike)
12) Price (Only 4 payments of $39.95.)

A recent survey found that 48% of Detroit inner city billboards were for alcohol or tobacco products versus 24% of the ads in a nearby white neighborhood.

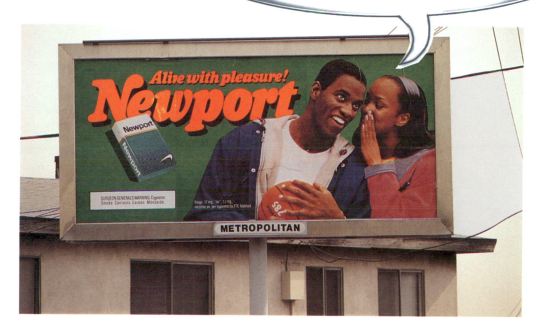

Group Exercise 1: Collect a dozen or more print ads and identify which advertising techniques listed above are used in the ads. Discuss which of the techniques are more likely to get the attention of your group.

Group Exercise 2: In small groups, analyze what you are wearing and why you are wearing it. How do the media or other students influence your clothing decisions?

Personal Inquiry: Describe how much and in what ways you might have been influenced by music, music videos, and other media portrayals of the following:

How you display sexual interest in another person;
How you have defined your attitude and "look."

CHAPTER 14

Free To Choose
The Compulsivity Of Tobacco

This chapter looks at tobacco use and abuse and then
encourages the design of projects that will
help reduce smoking.

Doonesbury

DOONESBURY Copyright 1993 G.B. Trudeau. Reprinted with permission of
UNIVERSAL PRESS SYNDICATE. All rights reserved.

❝ *"Nicotine is not only a very fine
drug, but the technique of administration by smoking has distinct psychological
advantages. . . Smoking is a habit of addiction."*

*Sir Charles Ellis, Scientific Advisor to
British-American Tobacco Co., 1962*

In Congressional hearings, advertisers
objected to proposed legislation to ban cigarette
advertising on radio and TV. They framed their
objections to a ban in terms of the themes "freedom
of choice" and "freedom to determine the course of
our own lives." And while people do have a choice
about whether to start, they find it extremely difficult
to quit given the highly addicting properties of nicotine. Advertising continues to present tobacco products as an adult thing to do, a source of pleasure, or
a ticket to "Marlboro Country," avoiding the fact that
extensive research has found that tobacco is one of
the most addictive psychoactive drugs.

What do people get from cigarettes?

- The average cigarette delivers 1 milligram of
  nicotine. Chain smokers might get their nicotine level up to 6 milligrams; 70 milligrams is
  fatal.
- The nicotine in the first cigarette of the day rais-
  es heart rate an average of 10-20 beats per
  minute and blood pressure 5-10 points.
- As the nicotine level rises, it has a calming
  effect because it releases endorphins, the
  body's natural tranquilizers.

A major reason for compulsive use of nicotine
is the urge to maintain a certain nicotine level in the
bloodstream. When the nicotine level drops below a
certain point, craving becomes intense, the user can
become irritable, nervous, and discontent and pro-
ceed to smoke, chew, or use snuff.

One of the strongest indications that tobacco
is addicting is the fact that of the 3 1/2 million high
school students who smoke, 70% do so on a daily
basis. With any other psychoactive drug, only 10-
20% of all users take the drug on a regular or daily
basis. High daily use is often a function of price,
availability, and legality, but even with alcohol, a
legal drug, only 20% of all drinkers use on a daily
basis.

Fortunately, a recent study shows that 75% of
full-time college students do not smoke regularly,
continuing an 18-year trend.

Exercises Chapter 14

Workbook Exercise 1: To the following suggestions for quitting smoking, add 5 of your own.

- Tell everyone you're quitting so that your pride is at stake.
- Avoid triggers such as coffee, alcohol, and smoking settings, e.g., bars.
- Remind yourself you'll live longer and smell better.
- Be aware of the danger of relapses which usually happen after about a month, often from overconfidence.
- Join a Smoke Enders type group.
- Consider nicotine replacements such as patches or gum.

EXERCISE

1

1) _____

2) _____

3) _____

4) _____

5) _____

Smokers have been trying to quit for scores of years. Early patent medicines such as NO-TO-BAC have given way to nicotine patches and other therapies. (William Hefland Collection, New York).

❝ "I started smoking when I was 15 and got up to a couple of packs a day. First time I quit for any length of time, I had a cold and couldn't breathe too well. That lasted until the end of my cold, 10 days. The fourth time I quit, it lasted a year and a half. At a bar with some friends, I smoked a couple of cigarettes and within a week, I was back to 2 packs. The sixth time I quit, I had been to a health fair and saw a specimen of a dead smoker's lung, black and gritty. It's been 28 years since my last cigarette, but I know that I could be back to 2 packs within weeks because that smoking habit was literally burned into my brain, probably within 3 months of starting."

53-year-old recovering smoker

EXERCISE

2

Workbook Exercise 2: Most people who finally quit try many times before they succeed. To the suggestions listed below, add 5 ways to lessen the health risk if someone has difficulty quitting smoking.

- Smoke only 1/2 or 2/3 of a cigarette, since the highest concentration of nicotine and tars accumulate at the end.
- Inhale less; you'll get the flavor but not bring smoke to the lungs.
- Buy low tar and nicotine cigarettes, but don't increase the amount you smoke.

1) _____
_____

2) _____
_____

3) _____
_____

4) _____
_____

5) _____
_____

EXERCISE

3

Workbook Exercise 3: List 5 things you could say to or do for a younger sibling or friend to keep him or her from beginning to smoke.

1) _____
_____

2) _____
_____

3) _____
_____

4) _____
_____

5) _____
_____

> ❝ "Think of the cigarette pack as a storage container for a day's supply of nicotine. Think of the cigarette as a dispenser for a dose unit of nicotine."
> Tobacco industry internal memo, 1972

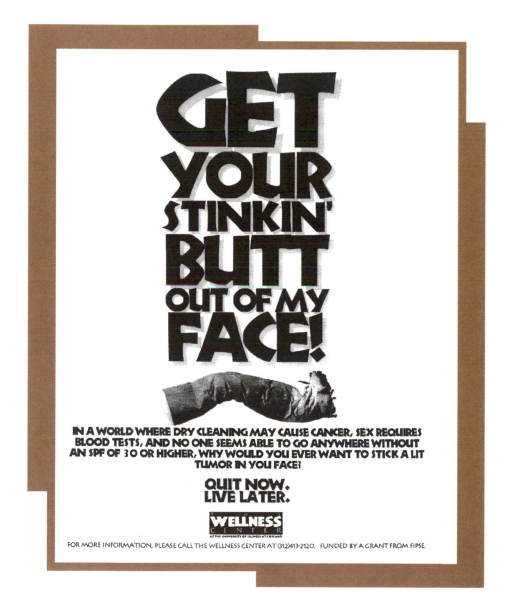

GET YOUR STINKIN' BUTT OUT OF MY FACE!

IN A WORLD WHERE DRY CLEANING MAY CAUSE CANCER, SEX REQUIRES BLOOD TESTS, AND NO ONE SEEMS ABLE TO GO ANYWHERE WITHOUT AN SPF OF 30 OR HIGHER, WHY WOULD YOU EVER WANT TO STICK A LIT TUMOR IN YOU FACE?

QUIT NOW.
LIVE LATER.

WELLNESS CENTER
AT THE UNIVERSITY OF ILLINOIS AT CHICAGO

FOR MORE INFORMATION, PLEASE CALL THE WELLNESS CENTER AT (312)413-2120. FUNDED BY A GRANT FROM FIPSE.

Group Exercise: Divide into groups of 5 and have each group design an anti-smoking print ad or a 30-second radio ad. Design these ads with some of these thoughts in mind:

- 90% of all adult smokers started in their teens.
- 80% of all teen smokers wish they had never started.
- 78% of all adult smokers want to quit.
- 78% of all smokers think nicotine is addicting.
- Advertisers cynically tout smoking as a rite of passage for teenagers.

Personal Inquiry: Write an account of a friend's or your own tobacco history including why the first cigarette was smoked or the first chew taken, what level of use was reached, and whether there was a desire or attempt to stop. If attempts were made, how many were there, and if the final attempt was successful, how was it accomplished?

CHAPTER 15

RITES OF PASSAGE

Drugs And Maturation

After considering the connections between emotional growth
and the use of alcohol and other drugs, this chapter asks
you to explore your concept of adulthood.

DOONESBURY ©1992 G.B. Trudeau. Reprinted with permission of
UNIVERSAL PRESS SYNDICATE. All rights reserved.

There are physical rites of passage to adulthood that include the sexual changes of puberty. There are legal rites of passage including the right to drive, the right to vote at 18, the age requirements for military service, signing a contract, and consensual sex. There are social rites of passage such as going to college, getting a job, or buying a car. And in many societies, some people identify drug use, especially use of alcohol, tobacco, and marijuana, with adulthood, partly because of definitions of "legal age" and partly because of cultural assumptions about what constitutes adult behavior and adult privileges. Some people use drugs as highly visible assertions of independence and adult status. Underage drinking and smoking can also be used as acts of defiance towards authority.

The irony of using alcohol and other drugs as a signal of adulthood is that their effects on emotion, mood, and thinking slow down the psychological and social developmental process. If individuals come to rely on alcohol and other drugs (or the compulsive use of food, sex, gambling) to get through difficult times, they may not develop the ability to cope with difficult situations without those substances or behaviors.

> "I got around my problems through the use of beer and marijuana. Unfortunately, I found out that once you stop, you actually return to the level of emotional stability that you were at when you started. So it was really a scary thing. I felt like I was 12 or 13 again, and I had all these hangups and problems dealing with life."
>
> 25-year-old salesman

EXERCISE

1

Workbook Exercise 1: In an attempt to help the process of growing into adulthood, Ron Johnson of Los Angeles developed "The 10 Steps - Rites of Passage Program" to help people judge their growth. This list is adapted from his ideas. Pick 4 categories that you feel most strongly about and describe something specific you are doing or could do to further your growth.

Physical: Make your health, nutrition, hygiene, and physical activities your personal responsibility.

Mental: Develop the thirst and the skills for the acquisition of knowledge.

Emotional: Learn to identify feelings, learn the difference between responses and reactions, reinforce emotional honesty with self and others.

Spiritual: Explore the connection between self and a higher power, value, or goal.

Social: Make sure your family, community, and even country benefit from your presence.

Personal: Accept that life can seem hard and unfair, but your ability to love, struggle, and overcome obstacles produces the fruits of your labor and gives you the faith to carry on.

Cultural: Accept that your culture is the framework for your values, perceptions, and interactions in this world.

Historical: Learn of your heritage since it inspires growth and reinforces the struggle for individual and community development.

Political: Take an active role in your community or government.

Economic: Take the responsibility of establishing and maintaining a sound economic foundation as a means to becoming an adult and building a family.

1) _____

2) _____

3) _____

4) _____

Workbook Exercise 2: Describe how people at different ages might define adult use of alcohol. For example, a junior high school student might define it by the way his parents use it or might consider getting high as the adult thing to do.

A high school senior: _____

_____

_____

_____

A college freshman: _____

_____

_____

A college senior: _____

_____

_____

A 30-year-old married man or woman: _____

_____

_____

_____

Workbook Exercise 3: List 5 different activities that you did over the past week that you consider a reflection of your maturity.

1) _____

_____

2) _____

_____

3) _____

_____

4) _____

_____

5) _____

_____

Group Exercise: Part of the passage to adulthood is learning ways to feel and control one's emotions. In small groups, discuss the ways people can develop the following skills:

1) Having a moderate to high tolerance for frustration;
2) Being able to work towards a goal without constant encouragement and guidance;
3) Accepting consequences for one's actions;
4) Being willing to ask for help and not feel resentful;
5) Accepting limits, rules, norms;
6) Experiencing feelings but not continuously acting them out;
7) Feeling moods more deeply but not changing them rapidly;
8) Being able to accept rejection;
9) Living in the present but being interested in the past and future;
10) Accepting personal responsibility for one's own future;
11) Being willing to stop something pleasurable if it is bad for physical, mental, or spiritual health;
12) Seeing both sides of an issue and accepting differing opinions.

Courtesy of SOSC Publications

PI **Personal Inquiry:** Which responsibilities of adulthood are you looking forward to and which ones would you rather not have to deal with?

FOR BETTER OR FOR WORSE © Lynn Johnson Prod., Inc.
Reprinted with permission of UNIVERSAL PRESS SYNDICATE. All Rights Reserved.

Resiliency

My first memory of violence and drugs was in my infancy, being held up as a shield for protection against my raging drunk father beating up my mother. Her thinking was that holding me up might stop him. I just remember being pummeled and not much more than that.

Raised in the Philadelphia slums, I got many beatings from my brothers who were older and had many beatings on the streets and alleys. I learned to fight as well as I could. I progressed into gangs and weapons, knives and chains mostly. In time, I turned into an excellent fighter and took pride in winning and being a gang leader.

In '67, I was drafted into the Army, right in time for the Viet Nam Tet offensive. I fought through endless months of heavy combat. Multiple thousands of persons died in the mass slaughter of human wave attacks. I was in some of the biggest battles of the Viet Nam War, Phu Bai, Wai City, Ashah Valley, LZ Sally, Rock Pile, LZ Stud, and Cason. It was more insane than being raised up in the violence of the city.

Toward the end of my tour, I was numb to pain and death; life had very little meaning. Back on Phu Bai base, some months later when the war had calmed down and new replacements came in, something was pushing me on to maintain the violence. I'd crawl through the barbed wire, out through the perimeter, to look for an enemy. I was split in my mind whether to go back to the States or stay in Viet Nam. All the carnage started to warp my ability to feel human suffering. I had the sense of being on automatic pilot with the senses of a shark on the smell of blood. When the orders came through to go back to the States, I was indifferent and got on the plane, and 3 days later I was in California.

The hippie movement of '69 was on. It was free love and bright colors in dress and doing acid. I felt a feeling of warmth take over and a sense of belonging rather than killing. It was very confusing. The non-violence was a relief and I welcomed it. The hippie movement was fine for a while, but was lacking in true love and compassion, in that it was a movement and wasn't personal. I was looking for one-on-one commitment and long-term involvement, whereas the movement was a short-lived substitute for those things.

Relationships don't happen instantly for most people, and there are disapointments, but for me to give up looking for love would have been a sentence back to darkness. Over time, I made caring relationships. I think this is the root of what made the difference between choosing violence and drugs, or not.

In violence and drug usage there's excitement, there's a numbness of feeling of things you want to forget. Some of the effects you try for you get, but it's completely lacking in warmth, caring and love. If those things aren't important to you, you'll go on until it (violence or drugs) kills you or somebody stops you; you'll miss what life should be. The values of the individual will determine the outcome.

People are into vast delusions. They pretend that they don't see the outcome. They just see what they want to see. When the shit hits the fan, it's not how they thought it would be. You can get under the delusion that if you do a violent act, you'll feel better and be stronger and have control over your life. But after the violent act, the feeling's still there and the act didn't quench your thirst. So you can delude yourself again and fall into a bot-tomless pit, or you can take charge of your life and try not to have your bad feelings throw you off track.

When the anger comes up, I mull the feelings over in my mind. I figure out all the aspects and the consequences, on multiple planes, then the effect it will have on what I hold dear in my life and my responsibilities to others. A fast reaction isn't always the reaction that will win, but could be the one that will do you in. In short, you have to want to care and be cared for.

"I'd Like To Get To Know You"

Relationships, Drugs, And Social Skills

Strong social skills help avoid reliance on alcohol and drugs as an aid in relationships or as a focus for social occasions.

THE FAR SIDE By GARY LARSON

© 1988 FarWorks, Inc./Dist. by Universal Press Syndicate

"Yeah, yeah, buddy, I've heard it all before: You've just metamorphosed and you've got 24 hours to find a mate and breed before you die. . . . Well, buzz off!"

The FAR SIDE by GARY LARSON © 1994 FARWORKS, INC./ Dist. by UNIVERSAL PRESS SYNDICATE. Reprinted with permission. All rights reserved.

By the age of 20, most men and women have the ability to connect with others in a confident, responsive, and mutually satisfying way. Some, however, may come to rely on alcohol or other drugs to facilitate social encounters. Feeling socially uncomfortable, they find that certain substances lower inhibitions, overcome shyness, and chemically instill confidence. However, if the use continues, there is a risk that social skills may never fully develop.

In fact, a person may become so psychologically dependent on substances that every social occasion seems to require use. Moreover, by relying on alcohol and drugs, a person tends to develop a circle of companions who encourage use and downplay negative consequences. Because of the lowering of inhibitions, use may result in risky behavior, unplanned or unwanted sex, and even date or acquaintance rape. If the drinking continues, getting smashed may be the purpose of every social experience. Drinking games may then become the focus of an evening's events, and getting drunk, quickly or slowly, the prime directive.

Because people's social skills differ greatly, some who find themselves alone and unable to connect with others may use substances as consolation for loneliness, shyness, rejection, and further diminish their feelings of self-worth, beginning a truly self-destructive cycle.

> " "The cocaine made me feel as if I could do anything, could say anything. It made me confident. And then when I was using the alcohol to come down from the coke, it reduced my inhibitions so I could say even more. I was brave. Then when I cleaned up my act, people would tell me how much they liked the way I was now...how fantastic the change was. I wonder what I really did when loaded because obviously, my perception of what and how I did had little to do with reality."
>
> 27-year-old recovering cocaine addict

EXERCISE

1

Workbook Exercise 1:   Complete 3 of the following activities and write up the outcome. What did you expect to happen? What happened? What are your expectations for a similar experience in the future?

1) Initiate a conversation with someone of the opposite sex you have not spoken with before.

_____

_____

_____

_____

_____

_____

2) Schedule a conference with one of your instructors, one whom you have not met with before.

_____

_____

_____

_____

_____

_____

3) Ask directions of someone and then engage the person in conversation for at least 3 minutes (in the library, around campus, etc.).

_____

_____

_____

_____

_____

_____

(Workbook Exercise 1, continued on next page)

(Workbook Exercise 1, continued)

4) Either give a compliment to someone or apologize to a friend and admit you were wrong.

_____

_____

_____

_____

_____

_____

_____

_____

5) Tell someone about an emotion you are feeling.

_____

_____

_____

_____

_____

_____

_____

_____

> ❝ "The best party we had all year was a pot-luck. There was alcohol there, but it wasn't the focus of the evening. No one got drunk or sick. People were so surprised. In fact, months later, this was the party everyone was still talking about."
>
> Lewis and Clark College sophomore

EXERCISE 2

Workbook Exercise 2: Good friendships can last a lifetime. Make a list of the qualities that make a good friendship. Then add what responsibilities each person in a relationship has to keep a friendship strong.

_____

_____

_____

_____

_____

_____

_____

_____

_____

_____

Group Exercise 1: In small groups, discuss expectations of alcohol use in the following circumstances:

1) An all-male group in a study session or a Monday Night Football party;
2) An all-female group in a study session or out for lunch;
3) A mixed group on a double date or at a family gathering.

Specify the typical alcoholic drinks, the usual location, and the kinds of behavior that are tolerated and not tolerated.

Group Exercise 2: Besides maintaining eye contact, being willing to listen, or being prepared with small talk, what other conversational or social hints can the group offer to make socializing easy, pleasant, and mutually satisfying?

Group Exercise 3: In small groups, discuss appropriate and inappropriate ways to do the following:

1) Introduce yourself to a person you have not met.
2) Join a group of at least 2 people and enter the conversation.
3) Invite someone to join in a conversation you are engaged in.
4) Re-engage someone in conversation after 20 minutes, asking to be reminded of her or his name.
5) Break off a conversation with someone who is being obnoxious.
6) Find a mutual interest and make a date to explore that interest.

 Personal Inquiry: Rate yourself on how often you use the following social skills:

	Often	Sometimes	Never
Initiate conversations	____	____	____
Carry on conversations	____	____	____
Give compliments	____	____	____
Receive compliments	____	____	____
Express an emotion	____	____	____
Refuse an unreasonable request	____	____	____
Ask a stranger a question	____	____	____

Write about 2 skills that you consider your strengths.

What Are The Chances?
Sexually Transmitted Diseases And HIV

To protect yourself and your friends, it is important to lessen the risks of combining psychoactive substances and sexual activity.

Sculpture by Auguste Ottin

The very nature of psychoactive drugs alters the brain and can impair judgment. These psychoactive substances, combined with sexual desire and activity, mute or dull that part of the brain that helps us reason or discriminate. Cautionary self-statements such as "What do I know about this person?" "Use a condom," "I could end up a father," "I could get pregnant," or simply, "Don't do it!" get lost in that anticipation of pleasure and the alteration of brain chemistry.

The challenge is to control alcohol or other drug use when sexual activity is involved and anticipate your behavior beforehand so that when you get in that situation, you will be able to protect yourself. As a familiar motto says, "Be prepared." Be prepared with enough money to get back home. Be prepared with a condom and other protection. Be prepared to refuse.

Among heavy college drinkers (5 or more drinks in a row), 41% had unplanned sex and 22% had unprotected sex — sex which can lead to pregnancy or a sexually transmitted disease (STD) including HIV disease.

Although HIV disease gets most of the headlines, other STD's are much more prevalent. Almost half of all sexually active teenagers have chlamydia, an infection of the urethra and surrounding tissues in men and infection of the urethra, cervix, fallopian tubes, uterus, and ovaries in women. About 20% of all sexually active men and women have genital herpes, a virus that causes open, cold-sore-like lesions.

In the United States, in 1992, the Centers for Disease Control reported:

491,000	new cases		of gonorrhea;
362,000	"	"	of chlamydia;
100,000	"	"	of HIV infection (which will lead to AIDS);
21,000	"	"	of hepatitis B;
34,179	"	"	of primary and secondary syphilis;
17,000	"	"	of genital herpes;
16,600	"	"	of genital warts.

In addition, in 1993, 28% of all pregnancies and a staggering 84% of all teen pregnancies were outside of marriage.

Workbook Exercise 1: List 5 precautions an individual can take before or during a date that will keep him or her from risky sexual activity (e.g., double-date with someone you trust if you don't know your date).

EXERCISE

1

1) _____
_____
_____
_____

2) _____
_____
_____

3) _____
_____
_____

4) _____
_____
_____

> " "I always thought that if you had any STD, you would know. Unfortunately, I got chlamydia and didn't have symptoms. I not only gave it to my fiancee, but the chlamydia became PID [pelvic inflammatory disease]. I let it go too long and that made it impossible for me to have children. Near as I could figure, my lifetime of problems came from one night when I thought, `What are the chances?'"
>
> 28-year-old artist

EXERCISE 2

Workbook Exercise 2: A student who prefers sex "au naturelle" and refuses to use condoms, had 5 partners in 1 year. He/she develops chlamydia during that year. Describe the potential problems (e.g., infectiousness, social reaction, telling lovers).

_____
_____
_____
_____
_____
_____

EXERCISE 3

Workbook Exercise 3: You think your younger brother or sister is already sexually active. What would you say to help her/him avoid STD's and an unwanted pregnancy? How would you broach the subject? What would you say about abstinence? Include advantages and disadvantages.

_____
_____
_____
_____
_____
_____
_____
_____
_____
_____
_____
_____
_____
_____
_____

- **Chlamydia:** This is a bacterial infection of the urethra and surrounding tissues in men and the urethra, cervix, and pelvic structures in women.
- **Pelvic Inflammatory Disease (PID):** This is an infection which spreads into the pelvic structures (the uterus, fallopian tubes, and ovaries); a potential cause of infertility.
- **Human Papilloma Virus (HPV):** This virus is identified with cellular changes on a woman's Pap smear. It can lead to pre-cancerous changes. (See genital warts.)
- **Genital warts:** Viral in origin, these pinkish white singular bumps or clusters of tissue in a cauliflower form are related to HPV.
- **Gonorrhea:** This common bacterial infection causes a yellow, mucous-like discharge and painful urination in men; women generally have no symptoms, but this infection can result in sterility if not treated.
- **Genital herpes:** This common viral infection produces blister-like sores in the genital region.
- **Syphilis:** This bacterial infection has 3 phases which can cause irreversible tissue damage and even lead to insanity.
- **Pubic lice (crabs):** These are parasitic insects that live in the pubic hair and tissue where they lay eggs and cause intense itching.
- **HIV Disease:** Blood-borne viral disease which, over the years, attacks the immune system and causes many illnesses, progressing to AIDS and premature death.

GROUP EXERCISE

Group Exercise 1: In small groups, discuss or role-play 1 of the following scenarios. Continue the discussion or role-playing until the outcome satisfies you.

1) You are planning a committed relationship with someone, and you need to know whether he or she has a sexually transmitted disease. Develop a scenario where the subject is brought up and discussed.

2) You do not wish to have sex although you feel your date is expecting it. You are afraid to say something. Think of a way to refuse effectively if asked.

3) You plan to be intimate with someone so you want to bring up the subject of pregnancy and protection.

4) You find out you have a sexually transmitted disease and you want to tell your partner so that anyone who may have been infected can get treatment.

 Personal Inquiry:

Describe ways to be sexually intimate or physically affectionate without having sexual intercourse or an exchange of body fluids.

CHAPTER 18

Protecting Yourself
Drugs, Anger, And Violence

Drugs, anger, and violence affect victims, perpetrators, and bystanders as well
as their relatives and friends. Preventative and
protective measures can be taken by each.

Journey of the Wounded Healer, 1984-85 by Alex Grey

Do drugs cause anger and violent behavior? We know that drugs, and especially alcohol,
often accompany violence, but the exact connection is still undetermined. The question of drugs
revolves around the relationship between chemically-induced behavior and a learned or cultural-
ly-influenced behavior. The outcome is also very dependent on the amount taken and the time-
frame of use.

- There are person-substance interactions: alcohol lowers inhibitions, so if a person has suppressed anger and violent tendencies, alcohol can release restraints on that anger and
  aggression. People who ordinarily don't fight, batter spouses, abuse children, or assault
  strangers, may do so when drunk or loaded. Strong stimulants, on the other hand, directly
  stimulate the fright, fight, flight center, often inciting one or all of those feelings.
- There are person-place interactions: some people become liable to anger or violent behavior
  only if they use in places such as a heavy metal bar, sporting event, fraternity party, or even
  a family reunion.
- The violence potential of drugs can also be culture specific: the tolerance of drinking and fighting is greater in the U.S. than in some Asian cultures.
- Then there is an economic component: some resort to crime and violence in order to support
  a habit or as part of the activity involved in the distribution of drugs.

Workbook Exercise 1:   Discuss how a potential perpetrator, victim, and bystander might respond to avoid violent outcomes in the following scenarios.

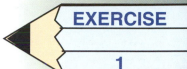

EXERCISE

1

Scenario 1: Both people have been drinking steadily all evening. The male begins pulling his date down the hall towards a bedroom. A friend notices that she seems reluctant, pulls away, and shakes her head. At this point, what could each person do to prevent a possibly violent outcome?

Potential perpetrator: _____

_____

_____

_____

Potential victim: _____

_____

_____

_____

Potential bystander(s): _____

_____

_____

_____

Scenario 2: Three teammates go out to a bar. During the evening, 1 teammate is insulted coming back from the restroom. Several people at the bar overhear the insult. What can each participant do to prevent possible violence?

Potential perpetrator: _____

_____

_____

_____

Potential victim: _____

_____

_____

_____

Potential bystander(s): _____

_____

_____

_____

FYI   In juvenile detention halls as well as adult prisons, the vast majority of those arrested were under the influence of alcohol or other drugs when they committed their crime.

FYI **Anger Management:** Anger is a legitimate emotion which can be positive and useful. It can be a survival mechanism, an opportunity to communicate, a motivator, a means of protecting one's self-worth. Anger is difficult to deflect or express in a controlled manner. Nevertheless, anger need not be acted out or cause harm. Anger control is possible. Unfortunately, the use of drugs disrupts the normal internal controls. In addition, a certain percentage of alcohol and drug abusers have personality disorders which make control of anger and emotions extremely difficult, especially when high.

EXERCISE

2

Workbook Exercise 2: Discuss a situation when someone became very angry. Discuss how the anger was or could have been self-affirming, protective, positive. Then discuss how the anger was or could have become aggressive, dangerous, and destructive. Finally, describe the actual outcome.

Situation: _____

_____

_____

Constructive potential: _____

_____

_____

Negative potential: _____

_____

_____

Actual outcome: _____

_____

_____

What do you now think and feel about the experience? _____

_____

_____

FYI Fifty percent of battered wives report that their husbands were drinking when the assault began. Remember, **absolutely no one has the legal or moral right to harm you physically!**

If you think you are going to be physically attacked by a stranger or someone you know:
- Plan your escape.
- Get away quickly.

If you are attacked:
- Don't think the initial attack was an isolated incident and will not continue; try to escape.
- Get legal, medical, and/or psychological help.
- Recognize that you are not responsible for the attack; it's not your fault.

Group Exercise 1: In groups of 3 or 4 people, devise a scenario involving drinking and anger and present it to the large group for discussion. Describe the situation and then the specific options open to the angry person, the person who is the object of the anger, and bystanders. Also discuss the effect of that anger on the relatives and friends of the people involved.

Group Exercise 2: In a large group format, discuss and provide specific examples for

- What encourages and what restrains violence during drinking events;
- What is likely to escalate routine disagreements and conflicts into hostile, angry aggression;
- What is likely to defuse tense situations or discourage aggressive outbursts.

For the above topics, provide specific examples.

FYI A recent study of deans of students found that about half cited acquaintance rape along with violence as the most common campus problems associated with alcohol or other drug use. About 75% of acquaintance rapes involve drinking by the victim, the perpetrator, or both.

To avoid date rape:

- Date in a group until you know the person.
- Don't go somewhere unfamiliar or far away until you know a person.
- Limit alcohol and other drug influences.
- Find a safe, neutral place for first encounters — a restaurant or movie.
- Don't assume that because you think you "know" someone that you are safe.
- Say "No" clearly, and keep repeating it if you do not want to engage in sex. If you aren't being heard, get out of there fast.

PI **Personal Inquiry:** Have you ever lost control, assaulted someone, or been assaulted during or after drinking, or witnessed such an assault? Thinking over the experience now, what could have been done to avoid or lessen the harm done?

Looking Out For Yourself

Alcohol And Harm Reduction

Although alcohol is widely used and readily available without prescription,
there are ways of minimizing risks and reducing harm
for the occasional, social, and regular drinker.

Make not thyself helpless in drinking in the beer shop. For will not the words of [thy] report repeated slip out from { thy mouth } without { thy knowing } { that thou hast uttered them? } Falling down thy limbs will be broken, [and] no one will give thee { a hand [to help thee up] } as for thy companions in the swilling of beer, they will get up and say, " Outside with this drunkard."

This hieroglyphic from 1,500 B.C. advised moderation in drink as well as avoidance of other compulsive behaviors. Translation from Precepts of Ani, *World Health Organization*

The idea that "safe" or "responsible" drinking should be encouraged is debatable. Some say that since all use by minors is illegal, only non-use should be promoted and that even for adults, drinking involves risks. (Imagine a first-time drinker downing 2 quick beers and then driving.)

Others say that according to a 1994 NIH national survey, 3/4 of high school seniors drank in the last year; half were drunk at least once; 9/10 of college students drank during the last year; 4 out of 10 have had more than 5 drinks at a sitting. So, the argument goes, since that's the case, let's help people eliminate or reduce harmful consequences of their drinking, keeping in mind that for some people in some situations, there is no "safe" or "responsible" way of drinking.

There is probably no safe way to drink if you are pregnant, suicidal, very depressed, a recovering alcoholic, a recovering addict, taking certain prescription drugs, diabetic, suffering from a bad liver or from another specific medical condition. Furthermore, although people with serious drinking problems may be able to control their drinking for a short time, for them there is no safe way of drinking because any alcohol starts the craving and triggers relapse. They require professional counseling and treatment.

Workbook Exercise 1: If you drink or use, describe 5 situations in which you would avoid drinking or using. If you don't drink or use, give 5 reasons why you don't.

1) _____
_____
_____

2) _____
_____
_____

3) _____
_____
_____

4) _____
_____
_____

5) _____
_____
_____

Workbook Exercise 2: For either alcohol, caffeine, tobacco, or gambling, develop 3 harm reduction tactics. For example: Substance: caffeine — Tactic: If I'm going to drink more than 2 cups of caffeinated coffee, I make sure the rest are decaffeinated. I will also avoid caffeinated colas.

EXERCISE

2

Substance: _____

Tactic: _____
_____
_____
_____

Tactic: _____
_____
_____
_____

Tactic: _____
_____
_____
_____

EXERCISE 3

Workbook Exercise 3: Interview several people to collect 5 additional safe-drinking tips and the reasons for them.

Tip: _____

Reason: _____

_____

Tip: _____

Reason: _____

_____

Tip: _____

Reason: _____

_____

Tip: _____

Reason: _____

_____

Tip: _____

Reason: _____

_____

Group Exercise 1: In small groups, create 2 drinking scenarios that involve risk. Two small groups should then merge and describe their scenarios to each other and ask for solutions from the other group. Suggest how through either planning beforehand or by using appropriate actions or words, high risks could be avoided.

Example:
Scenario: It's your first month at college and some new-found friends are planning to get drunk bar-hopping.
Solution: Stay in a familiar neighborhood. Realize that you don't have to get drunk to go bar-hopping. Plan to alternate alcoholic and non-alcoholic beverages. Eat while you drink. Make sure you have enough money to get home.

Non-alcoholic beer and wine.

Group Exercise 2: Have pairs of students role play the following situations for a few minutes. Have the group as a whole evaluate the results and provide alternatives.

1) Give advice to a younger relative who is just starting to drink.

2) Get the keys from an obviously drunk friend who wants to drive home.

3) You are out drinking with 2 friends when their argument is about to turn into a fight. Say or do something to defuse the situation.

4) You are hosting a party and someone proposes playing a drinking game and you don't want to. Say or do something to keep from being involved or to keep the game from beginning.

5) Create your own scenario.

FYI Women not only process alcohol less efficiently than men, they also usually weigh less. For example, if a 125- pound woman goes out with a 175-pound man and they each have 4 drinks over a 2-hour period, his blood alcohol will be .07, legally sober, and the woman's will be .132, legally quite drunk.

P.I. **Personal Inquiry:** Describe an occasion when good harm-reduction planning saved you from grief (or could have).

Walk The Talk
Changing The Current Environment

Examining campus/community alcohol and other drug practices and then working to change them when necessary can help reduce the environmental pressure to use.

People not only can change their own behavior to lower their susceptibility to alcohol and other drug abuse, they can also work to change the campus or community with which they interact on a daily basis. For example,

- If most functions or parties on campus only serve beer, wine, coffee, and hard liquor, people who prefer water, soft drinks, or juice have limited choices.
- If there are few non-alcoholic recreational activities on or near campus, that too limits students' choices.
- If colleges or universities do not enforce their own policies on substance use and abuse, then an overly permissive attitude is fostered and the use of alcohol and other drugs usually increases.

On-campus advertisement for peer educator program for students helping other students.

Courtesy of the Wellness Center, University of Illinois at Chicago

On the other hand

- If campus policy designates some of the residence halls as alcohol-and drug-free, then those who choose not to use do not feel pressured or uncomfortable.
- If free bus service is offered to and from school games, those who do drink have a safe way home.
- If students and neighborhoods set up peer education programs, support groups, and other non-judgmental places to go for help and information, then students don't feel alone.

But what if some people say, "Well, if others want to drink or use dope, that's their problem, not mine"? Certainly, each person has the right to choose his or her own course in life, but alcohol and other drugs are not used in a vacuum, and the spillover effects of noise, violence, vandalism, and all the other associated problems are difficult to avoid.

Workbook Exercise 1: Summarize an instance when you contributed your time to a person or cause. For example: you tutored another student, you were a Big Brother or Big Sister, you worked on a political campaign, or you simply helped a friend.

What you did: _____

_____

_____

The outcome: _____

_____

_____

How you felt during and after: _____

_____

_____

Workbook Exercise 2: What non-alcohol/non-drug related area of your campus or community life needs improvement? How could you contribute? For example, if the residence hall looks a little to grungy in the morning, you could set up a schedule for volunteers to clean up halls and other common areas.

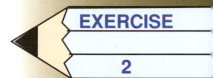

Area for improvement: _____

_____

_____

_____

What you could do: _____

_____

_____

_____

_____

> ❝ "I want to live in a better world. If people around me are better, that makes my experience better. What that means for me is doing some kind of campus or community service."
>
> S.F. State University sophomore

Workbook Exercise 3: Write a 30-second radio commercial, song or rap lyric for the campus radio station, a poem for the campus literary magazine, a letter to the editor for the campus paper, or design a poster that best expresses your views on alcohol or other drugs. You can aim it at a specific segment of the population if you wish.

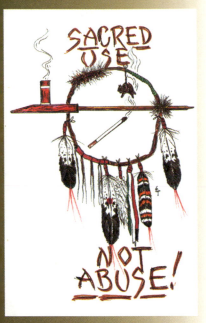

FYI Sixty-three percent of all fraternities self-insure through their own insurance organization. These fraternities' rules stipulate:

- No alcoholic beverages shall be purchased through chapter treasury.
- No bulk alcohol shall be purchased, e.g., kegs.
- No chapter members shall purchase for or serve minors.
- All rush activities must be dry.
- No member shall tolerate, permit or encourage, or participate in drinking games.

Group Exercise 1: Invite the dean of students, campus counselor, president of the student senate, director of student activities, or administrator in charge of alcohol and drug education to speak about the formal and informal campus policies relating to alcohol and other drugs.

Afterwards, in small groups, summarize those policies, briefly state your reasons for agreeing or disagreeing with them, and suggest policy revisions or policy additions.

Group Exercise 2: List campus or neighborhood activities and facilities which do not involve alcohol or other drugs or which promote natural highs. Then design a handbill, poster, or press release and persuade the campus paper to publish or post it in the cafeteria, dorms, student health center, etc.

This handbook was compiled by students at San Diego State University to let other students know about alcohol and drug laws, non-alcoholic events, where to get help, and other tips for their fellow students.

Courtesy of Louise Stanger, MSW

Personal Inquiry: Give the reasons why you would or wouldn't want to be involved with campus or community activities that might improve your school and neighborhood in relation to alcohol and drug problems. Discuss whether you think these kinds of activities make a difference.

PART III: HALTING THE PROGRESSION

The greater the amount of a drug used and the greater the frequency of use, the more quickly an individual can advance to unhealthy levels of use. Understanding the levels of drug use will help you or someone close to you understand methods for halting that progression.

After abstention or non-use, the levels of drug use can be divided into experimentation, social/recreational use, habituation, abuse, and addiction.

LEVELS OF USE

Experimentation: People don't seek out the drug. They are just curious and may take some to please friends or to satisfy curiosity. No patterns of use or negative consequences develop. Drug use is limited to a few exposures.

"When I was 15, I was on a camping trip with some other kids and they were all smokers. I had seen my mom smoke ever since I can remember, so I thought I'd give it a try. Talk about getting dizzy; I mean I thought I would pass out."

Social/recreational: Whether it's a beer at a restaurant, a joint with a friend, or a sniff of cocaine at a party, with social/recreational use, a person seeks out a drug and wants a certain effect from it, but there is no established pattern. Use is sporadic, and only occasionally has an impact on a person's life or health.

"I always liked the keggers at the frat parties. It made for a looser evening. I always thought I could score when booze was around. Not that I'm crazy over beer . . . I prefer wine . . . but the alcohol works."

Habituation: A definite pattern of use exists: the weekly TGIF high, the daily 6 cups of coffee, the pack-a-day habit. The regularity of use signals that a person has lost control over the drug. Regardless of the frequency, the definite pattern indicates that the drug has influence over the user.

"You would say that I was a habitual user, but I don't really think that's the case. So it is a habit. I like a drink. If the question is, could I go a day without having a drink, I think so, but I've never had a reason to try."

Drug abuse: When a drug is used despite negative consequences, that's drug abuse. It's abuse when someone uses amphetamines or even caffeine despite high blood pressure; LSD, despite mental instability; alcohol, despite being diabetic; cigarettes, despite asthma. If use goes on regardless of negative consequences to health, relationships, finances, legal implications, or emotional well-being, that's abuse.

"You know, people who do heroin aren't worried about dying and stuff because, like if 3 people die off a new batch of heroin, everybody wants to know where they are getting that heroin so they can go get some because it's the best. Just do a little less."

Addiction: The difference between abuse and addiction has to do with the degree of compulsion in the drug use. When someone spends most of the time getting, using, or thinking about the drug; when he or she disregards all health consequences; when, after withdrawal, the person still is compelled to use again because the psychoactive substance is still the most important thing in life, then that's addiction.

"After damning myself on a daily basis, after vowing to stop drinking, I would become transformed as evening approached. I would get wildly enthusiastic and anticipate another night of drinking. The self-hate would turn inside out, and become anticipatory pleasure. I was going to get loaded again."

CHAPTER 21-30 OVERVIEW

Chapters 21-29 focus on the ways of spotting problems with psychoactive substances — either your own or those of someone you know. These chapters also help develop skills in dealing with problems, either to halt their progression or, where dependency on substances is advanced, to know where to find and how to use support services.

Although recognizing substance abuse is difficult, even for professionals, there are some clear signs to be aware of **(Chapter 21)**. Most substance abuse involves protective mechanisms that are in place to guard the abuse and ensure it is not interrupted. One form this protective shield can take is denial, both by the person who abuses substances and by friends, family, and others **(Chapter 22)**. Another protective defense involves a variety of enabling behaviors which, in one way or another, allow substance abuse to continue **(Chapter 23)**.

The next 3 chapters present information and skills to keep abuse from progressing, either by coping with social pressures to use and abuse **(Chapter 24)**, by recognizing the compulsive use of food to manipulate mood **(Chapter 25)**, or by understanding the complex relationship between substances and psychological disorders **(Chapter 26)**.

Where problems persist and exceed one's abilities to cope, there exist both informal supports and self-help groups **(Chapter 27)**, as well as professional support services **(Chapter 28)**. The costs of using alcohol and other drugs are summarized in **(Chapter 29)**. The workbook concludes with a grand review and the expectation that the process of devising and practicing protective strategies.

Can You Tell? Should You Act?
Recognizing Signs
And Symptoms Of Substance Abuse

Recognizing signs and symptoms of excessive alcohol and other drug use can alert us to problems and the need to prevent escalation.

Overuse of alcohol and other psychoactive drugs is very difficult to spot. In fact, since denial of a problem is a hallmark of excessive drug use, most abusers quickly learn how to hide symptoms, so even addictive use can be hard to detect. In one study, a man deliberately exhibited the signs and symptoms of alcoholism when he went in for medical exams to see whether physicians could recognize alcoholism. Only 40% of the doctors connected the symptoms with alcoholism. Drug counselors have a much better chance of spotting abuse, but even they have to rely on urine tests to make sure their clients aren't using.

One clue to problematic use is a behavioral change in people you know. But behavior can vary widely from person to person, even for the same drug. One person will nod off after 2 hits of marijuana, another will raid the icebox. Behavior can also vary with amount. One person will be dancing after 5 drinks but in a fight 2 drinks later.

Then the question is, "If you suspect drug problems, should you do anything? If so, what?" Remember, unless you actually see someone take a drug and know what the drug is or smell alcohol on someone's breath, you can't be sure what is causing the behavioral or physical symptoms that alerted you in the first place. But you can use your intuition and make educated guesses.

Who me?

STURGEON

Exercises Chapter 21

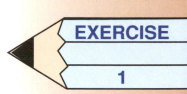

EXERCISE

1

Workbook Exercise 1: The following **behavioral signs** indicate that a person might be having problems with alcohol or other drugs. Add at least 4 more items that you would consider behavioral signs.

- Decline in grades or efficiency at work;
- More absences because of "not feeling good";
- Frequent struggles to stop using after 1 drink, 1 cigarette, or 1 hit;
- Outbursts of anger or irritability;
- Excessive time spent thinking about drinking or using;
- Deteriorating relationships with family members or isolation;
- Personality changes, sudden mood swings, or hostility;
- Wholesale changes in peer group;
- Paranoia and hyper-vigilance;
- Retorts like, "It's none of your business," when asked about drinking or drug use.

1) _____

2) _____

3) _____

4) _____

Workbook Exercise 2: The following **physical signs** indicate a person might be using a psychoactive substance. Some of the drugs that cause those effects are also listed. Add at least 5 more items that you think are physical signs of use and the drugs that cause these signs.

EXERCISE

2

- Pinpoint pupils (opiates like heroin or codeine);
- Dilated pupils (cocaine, amphetamines);
- Bloodshot eyes (marijuana, alcohol);
- Flushed complexion (alcohol, occasionally marijuana);
- Unhealthy weight loss (amphetamines, cocaine);
- Decline in dental health (amphetamines, alcohol);
- Pasty complexion (tobacco, amphetamines, cocaine);
- Tremors (most stimulants including caffeine).

1) _____

2) _____

3) _____

4) _____

5) _____

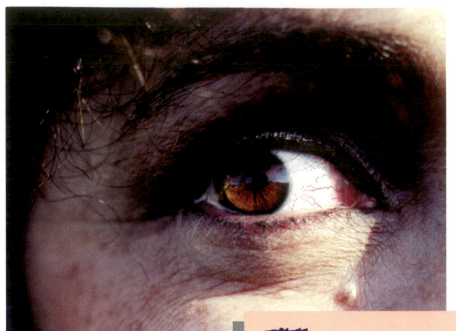

FYI Symptoms can be caused by withdrawal from a drug or alcohol as well as from the direct effects.

- Headache (alcohol hangover, caffeine withdrawal;
- Agitation (opiates, alcohol);
- Anger (almost any drug if you can't get it);
- Excess sweating (heroin or other opiate withdrawal);
- Depression (cocaine, tobacco);
- Irritability (sedatives).

EXERCISE

3

Workbook Exercise 3: Think of 2 or 3 people you know that you are fairly sure have or had a substance abuse problem. List the signs and symptoms you noticed which made you aware of the problem. Discuss whether you were able to pinpoint the substance used.

1) _____

_____

_____

_____

2) _____

_____

_____

_____

3) _____

_____

_____

_____

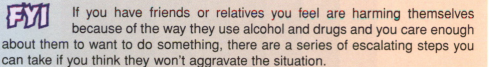 If you have friends or relatives you feel are harming themselves because of the way they use alcohol and drugs and you care enough about them to want to do something, there are a series of escalating steps you can take if you think they won't aggravate the situation.

- Talk with them and express friendship, affection, love, and concern. Don't confront someone who's drunk or high.
- Describe, precisely, the behaviors that concern you. Use "I" statements such as "I am concerned about your drinking," rather than "You drink too much." Don't speak when you are angry.
- Listen, listen, listen and be non-judgemental.
- Talk to their friends or relatives to make them aware and get them involved.
- Get someone they admire to talk to them.
- Find out what services are available and let them know.
- Go with them to an Alcoholics Anonymous, Alanon, Narcotics Anonymous meeting or any other self-help group that might be of service.
- Seek professional advice about how you could help them or yourself.
- Involve yourself in a professional intervention that might get them into treatment.

GROUP EXERCISE

Group Exercise : Explore possible responses for the following scenarios:

Scenario 1: Your roommate has been missing more classes lately, particularly the morning ones because of sleeping late. You can also smell alcohol on your roommate's breath, and you have become aware of his or her regular drinking patterns. Discuss what you would or could do, then have 2 students act out the dialogue. Discuss the results.

Scenario 2: You go home for the holidays and your 14-year-old sister seems more distant, she snaps at everyone, she doesn't seem to get nearly enough sleep, she's always 'getting something done,' and she's lost a little too much weight. Discuss what could be done and have 2 students act out the dialogue and discuss the results.

Personal Inquiry: Describe a friend or relative you saw going through problems with drug or alcohol use. Based on what you now know, what actions would you take?

Can You See Your Ears?
Overcoming Denial

Denial is a natural defense mechanism that can be protective or can be disabling.
The goal is to learn to recognize and overcome denial
that is disabling.

THE DAY THEY LEGALIZE DRUGS ISH THE DAY I LEAVE THE COUNTRY!

As a person's drug or alcohol use advances from experimentation to addiction, denial of the resulting problems can also advance and drift more and more to the unconscious level. The progression is often not noticed by family members and friends who may be immersed in their own denial. There are several kinds of denial which can serve either as a natural, protective reaction or as a barrier to dealing with reality.

■ **Suppression -** consciously avoid reality or painful memories, usually on a short-term basis: *"Can we change the subject? This is too embarrassing for me."*

■ **Repression -** unconsciously push aside painful memories that led to substance abuse and/or were caused by the abuse itself: *"I really haven't had any problems with drug use over the past few years. I just want to do drugs."*

■ **Rationalization -** use logical statements to give socially acceptable reasons to protect self-esteem: *"A couple of drinks calms me down after work."*

■ **Intellectualization -** develop abstract theories for actions and even describe one's own illness in the abstract: *"I know I'm drinking more but my liver produces extra enzymes to handle extra alcohol."*

■ **Displacement -** take suppressed feelings out on another: *"If the kids weren't screaming all the time and this place was not such a mess, I wouldn't have to drink."*

■ **Projection -** project own problems on others: *"You're the one who has a problem with my drinking, not me."*

Disabling denial can also also extend to any behavior with damaging consequences such as compulsive eating, gambling, and even shopping.

Workbook Exercise 1: Give examples of the 6 kinds of denial statements discussed on the previous page. They can be denials of any kind of behavior, ones that you have heard or used yourself. Then, think up an answer that a person could use to counteract that denial. Finally, describe 1 action that the person could actually do to face the situation.

For example:
> Statement: "It's what's inside that's important, not how I look on the outside."
> Answer: "That may be true, but at 240 pounds I start each relationship a few steps behind everyone else."
> Action: "I'll try to visualize myself as others see me."

EXERCISE 1

Rationalization

Statement: _____

_____

Answer: _____

_____

Action: _____

_____

Intellectualization

Statement: _____

_____

Answer: _____

_____

Action: _____

_____

Suppression

Statement: _____

_____

Answer: _____

_____

Action: _____

_____

(Workbook Exercise 1, continued on next page)

(Workbook Exercise 1, continued)

Repression

    Statement: _____

    _____

    Answer: _____

    _____

    Action: _____

    _____

Displacement

    Statement: _____

    _____

    Answer: _____

    _____

    Action: _____

    _____

Projection

    Statement: _____

    _____

    Answer: _____

    _____

    Action: _____

    _____

> "I'd go into a bar, and my rap was pretty good, <u>I thought</u>. A few times I'd pick up girls and bring them home to my house, and it was a big disappointment, to them, I mean. I was on Tuinals and Seconals. But the next night, I'd try again. I was scared to tell myself just how bad off I was."
>
> Recovering barbituate user

Overcoming disabling denial is the single hardest phase in reversing the progression of compulsive behavior. Denial acts like a special shield that protects one from frontal assaults. Each direct criticism or confrontation only serves to harden the shield, to protect the person from the pain of realizing how they have been harming themselves (and others).

Overcoming disabling denial is an internal process that begins when people
- hit a physical, emotional, and/or mental bottom which scares them into action;
- develop insight into their problem and try to correct their behavior;
- have an emotional or spiritual awakening which gives them the power to change the way they are living.

These methods of overcoming denial often require help from a friend, relative, or professional. However, asking for help is one of the hardest actions to take for someone in denial, but it is essential to overcoming substance abuse.

Group Exercise: In groups of 2 or 3, each person tells a denial story that describes what happened, whether or how realization came that there was a problem, and the outcome.

GROUP EXERCISE

PI **Personal Inquiry:** List past attitudes or activities which you had difficulty admitting harmed you (e.g., drinking or "front-loading" before you went to a party and getting very drunk). What kept you from admitting it and why? Next to that list, note what you did or could have done to change those behaviors.

Am I Helping Or Making It Worse?
Practical And Ethical Dilemmas Of Enabling

This chapter explores ethical issues involved with knowingly or unknowingly supporting another's alcohol/drug abuse.

People can contribute to and support someone else's substance abuse by ignoring or facilitating it, apologizing for it, denying abuse exists, attempting to control it, making excuses for it, or hoping it will go away. Often the unintended result of such efforts is to facilitate the abuse, allowing it to continue and thereby postponing intervention and getting the abuser into treatment. These are the different forms of supporting actions:

- **Inappropriate behavior**: e.g., urging others to go out drinking, buying alcohol for minors, or trying to get someone drunk or high just for fun. Harm may be done because someone might be in drug recovery, diabetic, a novice drinker, predisposed to addiction, or mentally unstable. These actions often result from simply not knowing or just not thinking about possible consequences until the damage is done.

- **Enabling behavior**: e.g., a person who cleans up the vomit on the floor rather than confront her roommate about her drinking; a co-captain who ignores a teammate's cocaine abuse; a father who pays higher insurance premiums after a son's DUI conviction. Enablers can be loyal, loving, well-intentioned friends and relatives. Even judges, social workers, doctors, and police can be enablers. Enablers want to soften the impact and reduce pain, and as a result, they end up shielding users from the consequences of their substance abuse.

- **Co-dependency** goes beyond enabling into the area of personality disorder. Co-dependents are so centered on the behavior and abusing actions of others that they tend to lose touch with their own identity, needs, and values. This loss of selfhood can even lead them to become alcohol or drug abusers to fill the emptiness. Co-dependency is a complex, clinical personality disorder that often requires professional treatment.

- **Co-addiction** is another behavior which often requires professional treatment. It occurs when a person begins heavy drinking or drug abuse in response to another person's habit (e.g., the man who begins heavy drinking to keep up with his girlfriend). One effect of co-addiction is to approve and support the abuse of others; a second is to become alcoholic or addicted oneself.

Workbook Exercise 1: Describe 4 kinds of behaviors relating to alcohol or drugs which you witnessed or heard about that you thought were **inappropriate**. Explain your reasons.

1) Behavior: _____

    Reasons: _____

    _____

2) Behavior: _____

    Reasons: _____

    _____

3) Behavior: _____

    Reasons: _____

    _____

4) Behavior: _____

    Reasons: _____

    _____

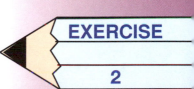

Workbook Exercise 2: Many behaviors "enable" people to use drugs or engage in risky activities more easily. Enabling can be active (a 20-year-old who gives his younger brother some marijuana) or passive (a coach who turns his back when athletes on his team use steroids). List 3 **enabling behaviors** that you've seen or engaged in and describe what could have been done to lessen the harm.

Example: Inappropriate behavior: sharing course notes with a roommate who misses classes because of hangovers.
Counter-behavior: telling the roommate, "Sorry, I'm not going to cover for you anymore. It's not doing either of us any good."

1) Behavior: _____

    _____

    Counter-behavior: _____

    _____

2) Behavior: _____

    _____

    Counter-behavior: _____

    _____

3) Behavior: _____

    _____

    Counter-behavior: _____

    _____

EXERCISE

3

Workbook Exercise 3: Many families or groups involved with enabling or **co-dependent** behavior have spoken or unspoken "rules" which guarantee that everyone will continue to do business as usual, not confront problems, and not take control of their lives. For 1-4, describe a more helpful alternative to the "enabling" rule. For 5-7, list other unspoken or spoken rules you have seen (or obeyed) and provide helpful alternatives.

Example:
Rule: Don't talk about problems.
Alternative: Have a specific time each day when parent and child, husband and wife, or roommates discuss problems.

1) Rule: Ignore or apologize to others for any unpleasant substance-related scene.

Alternative: _____

_____

_____

2) Rule: Don't express feelings openly.

Alternative: _____

_____

_____

3) Rule: Don't assert **your** needs or rights. (Note: this is different than being self-absorbed and demanding to the exclusion of others.)

Alternative: _____

_____

_____

4) Rule: Don't confront anyone or rock the boat.

Alternative: _____

_____

_____

5) Rule: _____

Alternative: _____

_____

_____

6) Rule: _____

Alternative: _____

_____

_____

7) Rule: _____

Alternative: _____

_____

Group Exercise 1: To decide to stop enabling someone's substance abuse, we may confront an ethical dilemma. (A dilemma exists when we are faced both with the necessity of acting and with the impossibility of acting in a way that honors competing obligations, ideals, or consequences. Conflicting loyalties, values, or probable outcomes seem so balanced that we can't be sure we are choosing the right thing, although we feel we **must** do something.)

In small groups, discuss the competing responsibilities and values for the following dilemmas. Then work out solutions and share them with the group as a whole.

1) Your friend does not have enough money to pay next semester's tuition, you do not have enough money to loan your friend, and your friend begins dealing drugs.

2) You are assistant manager at a local supermarket and a group of employees, one of whom got you the job, invites you to smoke "some pot" with them on their break.

3) On a visit home, you run into a friend who is crying and has bruises on her face. She says that her father has been drinking again but she's okay and she asks you not to get involved or say anything. She says the reason he did it was that he can't find a job and feels bad and if you interfere you will only make things worse.

4) Members of your fraternity, sorority, or social group are hosting keggers and parties with open bars in violation of local and national regulations.

5) You occasionally drink in your room with friends, but the hard partying in your dorm is waking you at night and interrupting your studying. You have heard others in the dorm grumble about the noise, smell, and arguing but so far nothing has happened. (You personally like some of the hard partyers.)

Group Exercise 2: In small groups, discuss what you wish people hadn't let you get away with in the past (e.g., being allowed to drink when I wanted rather than being taught how to drink).

Personal Inquiry: Summarize a difficult ethical decision you made concerning alcohol/drug use that involved enabling. Discuss whether you are satisfied with the outcome, and whether you might now make a different decision.

Standing Firm
Enhancing Refusal Skills

Destructive drinking or drug use pressures (spoken and unspoken) from friends, associates, and even family members can be counteracted with resistance skills.

THE FAR SIDE By GARY LARSON

Primitive fraternities

We humans are social beings. We seek each other out, take pleasure in one another's company, and find both comfort and reassurance by being part of a group. To stay a member of a group, we often do things to please others or to conform with our perception of others' expectations.

As we mature, those pressures remain and can be just as strong and compelling for college students, working adults, or those in the military as they are for young adolescents. The messages may be less direct, more subtle and more sophisticated, but they still urge us to yield to whatever happens to be the group's norms. A group of equals or people with common interests (peer group) may replace the family as the source of companionship, shared experience, and validation.

There can be trade-offs, though. If the peer group includes illicit drug use and excessive drinking, the benefits conferred by a group — companionship, talking, joking, having a good time — may be at the expense of safety, health, or personal values and beliefs. Peer pressure can take several forms.

- **Direct pressure** to use such as invitations to go out drinking; offering drinks or drugs; drinking contests or challenges;

- **Indirect pressure** to use such as boasting of drinking exploits and number of drinks consumed; glorifying illicit drug use and other risky behavior; memorializing occasions of abuse ("Thirsty Thursday"); ostracizing someone who doesn't use ("Whatta dork"); mocking or insulting someone who doesn't use ("What are you, a 'narc'?");

- **Self-imposed pressure** to use as a way of fitting in and being accepted, such as feeling you might be left out if you refuse; fear of embarrassment; not knowing how to refuse. (Internalizing group expectations is the most frequent and powerful source of peer pressure.)

> **FYI** Sometimes it's hard to refuse an offer to drink, use other drugs, or participate in some risky behavior. It takes planning beforehand. (For all you know, someone else who doesn't want to use may follow your lead.)
>
> Here are some resistance tactics:
>
> | Tactic: | Example: |
> |---|---|
> | ■ Propose a substitute. | "Let's work out instead." |
> | ■ Question motives. | "Just why are you trying to get me high?" |
> | ■ State obligations. | "Nope. I'm the designated driver." |
> | ■ State personal rules. | "I always stop at two." |
> | ■ Be direct. Simply refuse and offer no explanations. | "No. Thanks, anyway." |
> | ■ Make an exit. | "Gotta go to the bathroom." |
> | ■ Make a point. | "I did that in high school." |

Workbook Exercise 1: Add 5 more resistance tactics that you illustrate with examples.

EXERCISE 1

       Tactic: Example:

1) _____   _____

2) _____   _____

3) _____   _____

4) _____   _____

5) _____   _____

Workbook Exercise 2: Describe 3 occasions when you did something you really didn't want to do and didn't know how to refuse. Compose a refusal statement you would now use.

EXERCISE 2

Occasion 1: _____

_____

_____

Occasion 2: _____

_____

_____

Occasion 3: _____

_____

_____

Workbook Exercise 3: In the following situations, find ways to respond in order to keep your self-respect, be respectful of others, save face, have fun, keep your friends, and yet, avoid harm.

1) You are in a dorm room with some friends, sitting in a circle, and a "bong" is being passed around. It comes to you but you don't wish to smoke. You say/do the following:

_____

_____

_____

_____

_____

2) You are throwing a party which has gone on until all the alcohol has been consumed and several people are drunk. A guest comes up and says, "Let's go get some more brewskies." You say/do the following:

_____

_____

_____

_____

_____

3) A group of men/women are swapping stories about their sexual exploits with a person everyone knows. Not only do you not wish to join in but you feel uncomfortable about bad-mouthing this person. You say/do the following:

_____

_____

_____

_____

_____

4) Your study group has decided to pull an all-nighter, and the other members decide to take amphetamines to stay awake. You don't want to. You say/do the following:

_____

_____

_____

_____

_____

Group Exercise 1: Peer disapproval can be as strong an influence as peer approval. For example, if a majority of your friends disapprove of cocaine use, you probably will not experiment with it. Either on a separate sheet of paper or with a show of hands, take the following quiz. Tabulate and discuss the results.

		your friends would		
If you		approve	disapprove	be neutral
1) Dyed your hair		____	____	____
2) Smoked a pack a day		____	____	____
3) Pierced your nose		____	____	____
4) Got drunk regularly		____	____	____
5) Wore a tie or dress every day		____	____	____
6) Smoked marijuana		____	____	____
7) Took up hang gliding		____	____	____
8) Used cocaine		____	____	____

> ❝ "When I ask a friend if they plan to drink at a party and they say, 'I don't know,' they almost always end up drunk. If they make up their minds about how much they'll drink beforehand, they have a chance."
>
> Lewis and Clark junior

Group Exercise 2: People are sometimes influenced more often by unspoken than spoken pressure. Discuss the unspoken pressures at a party which might encourage certain dress styles, alcohol or drug use, sexual behavior, or even hair styles.

Personal Inquiry: Discuss whether you personally are most susceptible to direct pressure, indirect pressure, or self-imposed pressure to use psychoactive drugs or engage in sex.

Food and Mood
Eating Disorders

By recognizing that food (including caffeinated food and beverages) is often used in the same way as psychoactive drugs, we can make sure our eating patterns are not harming us physically and mentally.

*The per-capita consumption of soft drinks in America is **303** 12-oz. cans or bottles of soft drinks per year.*

When food is used solely to control moods rather than to satisfy physical hunger, then eating can harm one's health. Because certain foods and non-alcoholic drinks act on the same areas of the brain and the same neurotransmitters as many psychoactive drugs, they can affect one's emotions and physical states.

Overeating and compulsive overeating: For example, refined carbohydrates such as flour and sugar can stimulate a person, sedate them, or even induce a mild euphoria, much as alcohol does. Fats and oils are also concentrated energy sources that can give a fast energy rush and then sedate. Unfortunately, like the side effects of any psychoactive drug that is used too often or in excess, the side effects of overeating start to outweigh the benefits: sluggish feeling, dulled senses, bad complexion, body odor, disliking oneself, feeling depressed, or feeling out of control. Interestingly, since alcohol is a refined carbohydrate, many people with eating disorders also have problems controlling their use of alcohol.

Bulimia and anorexia: On the opposite side of the coin, insufficient nutrition can occur when someone overreacts to society's view of how a person should look. In its more serious manifestations, it can lead to bulimia (compulsive overeating followed, often, by vomiting or purging) or anorexia (eating minute amounts of food to the point of starvation). With both bulimia and anorexia, the compulsion to control one's life through the control of what one eats (or doesn't eat) is extremely strong.

> ❝ "Growing up in a home with a mother who had schizophrenia and a father who drank too much, I found that food would give me a safe haven from the emotional turmoil. The hamburgers, sugared colas, cheesecake, and fries were my carbohydrate shortcut to giving myself pleasure without having to depend on others. It took 100 or so diets, a lifetime of denial, and finally joining Overeaters Anonymous to begin to learn how to deal, in an adult way, with others."
>
> 184-lb. (formerly 270-lb.) compulsive overeater

> ❝ "I used to throw up 3 or 4 times a day, to keep my weight down after gorging myself. I couldn't control that lust for food. Since all I thought I had was my looks, I would go to any lengths to keep them. The funny thing was, I talked to some guy on the wrestling team and found out some of them were using vomiting to make their wrestling weight. Finally, I got to like myself at whatever weight I was and stopped purging."
>
> 23-year-old recovering from bulimia

Exercises Chapter 25

EXERCISE

1

Workbook Exercise 1: If you have an eating disorder, one of the most important things you can do is drastically reduce your intake of refined sugars and caffeinated beverages and foods. Too much sugar over a long period of time can trigger adult onset diabetes, compulsive eating and obesity, hypoglycemia, and a variety of illnesses. Excessive caffeine can trigger panic attacks and anxiety. A reasonable use of caffeine would be about **100 mg or less** in a day and a reasonable use of sugar would be **50 grams** (about 1 2/3 ounces) **or less** in a day. Using the charts below as well as the information on the packages themselves, approximate your daily intake of sugar and of caffeine.

Refined Sugar: Americans use about 120 pounds of various refined sugars per year or 150 grams (gm) per day.

Food	Sugar
1 cup Raisin Bran	19 gm
1 cup Wheaties	4 gm
1 cup Branola	30 gm
12-oz. can of soda	40 gm
2-oz. candy bar	30 gm
1 small cookie	5 gm
1 cup ice cream	30 gm
1 donut	25 gm
1 piece of cake	25 gm
1 cup spaghetti sauce	14 gm
1 cup pancake syrup	140 gm

Caffeine: Over 80% of Americans use caffeine regularly. The average intake in the U.S. is 200 milligrams (mg) per day.

Beverage/food	Caffeine
Demitasse espresso	200 mg
5-oz fresh drip coffee	150 mg
5-oz. percolated coffee	100 mg
12-oz. iced tea	70 mg
12-oz. soft drink, e.g., Coke, Pepsi (sugar or sugar-free)	50 mg
2-oz bar of chocolate	20 mg
5-oz cup of strong tea	70 mg
Decaffeinated coffee	3 mg
Over-the-counter medications (OTC)	
No-Doz	200 mg
Dexatrim	200 mg
Many OTC's	30 mg

Daily sugar intake _____ gm   Daily caffeine intake _____ mg

EXERCISE

2

Workbook Exercise 2: List 3 specific things people could do to reduce their intake of sugar and caffeine.

Example: Check food packages for sugar and caffeine content and select low-sugar, low-caffeine foods and beverages.

1) _____

_____

_____

2) _____

_____

_____

3) _____

_____

_____

EXERCISE

3

Workbook Exercise 3: People often use food or non-alcoholic drinks to enhance, change, or create a mood. Make a list of which food, if any, you use for these purposes.

Enhance a mood: _____

_____

Change a mood: _____

_____

Create a mood: _____

_____

EXERCISE

4

Workbook Exercise 4: It is often as difficult to intervene with someone who has a food problem as it is with someone who has an alcohol or drug problem. Why?

_____

_____

_____

_____

_____

_____

_____

_____

EXERCISE

5

Workbook Exercise 5: What are 3 things you could try in order to help someone with a mild food problem? (Remember, a serious eating disorder such as compulsive overeating, bulimia, or anorexia most often needs professional help or the use of a self-help group such as Overeaters Anonymous.)

Example: Don't keep offering high sugar or high fat foods to a friend.

1) _____

_____

2) _____

_____

3) _____

_____

FYI The following questions are samples of those used for self-assessment of whether a person is using alcohol compulsively. By making the word "food" interchangeable with "alcohol," it is possible to see the similarities between the 2 addictions.

1) Do you wish people would stop nagging you about your drinking/overeating?
2) Do you regularly use alcohol/food to calm yourself?
3) Is it hard to imagine a social occasion without alcohol/food?
4) Do you envy people who can drink/eat a lot without getting into trouble gaining weight?
5) Do you tell yourself you can stop drinking/overeating any time you want while drinking /overeating ?
6) Do you go on drinking/eating binges for no particular reason?
7) Does your alcohol/food obsession make you unhappy?

If you say yes to 3 or more questions, you might be a compulsive drinker/overeater.

❝ "I was addicted to not eating. It was the only way I had to control my life. Otherwise I was just a people-pleaser. I tried to be so, so perfect to please my parents, but yet I got off on saying no to people's concerns about getting me to eat. I think that physically, I was in a hazy, euphoric state from starving myself. I went to a clinic for 6 months where I had to break that loop in my brain which said I stunk and was no good. I find that by liking myself, I also can like others."

20-year-old recovering from anorexia

PI **Personal Inquiry:** Note any particular foods (e.g., chocolate, pasta, doughnuts) or eating behaviors (e.g., "I can refuse one piece of my binge food, I can't refuse the second.") which have affected you physically, mentally, or emotionally. If there are such foods or behaviors, write down 1 beginning step to change (e.g., making sure none of that binge food is in your apartment or dorm).

FYI In a recent study, researchers found that 50-60% of all manikins used to display clothing had the measurements of someone who was anorexic or starving to death.

Group Exercise: Since cultural and gender influences play a large part in our attitudes towards weight and appearance, try some role reversal. Have the women in the class make a list of comments they think men make about women's weight and appearance. Have the men make comments they think women make about men's weight and appearance. Write the responses on the board. Then have a discussion about the accuracy of each gender's perception of what the opposite sex says. Finally, talk about the reasons each side says what it does. If it is felt the comments are harmful, suggest ways to change those behaviors.

GROUP EXERCISE

Julie's Story

I grew up thinking that I was fat. When I was 8 years old, I thought I was too fat to wear a dress. Jeans and baggy shirts were all I would wear. By the time I was 14 years old, I felt so bad about my body that I started to throw up after meals. At first I would only make myself throw up a couple of times a week. After a while, it started to get pretty easy and I started to throw up whenever I thought I had eaten too much. It didn't take long before I would throw up after every meal or snack I had. I would sit in my room and finish off a box of cookies, a couple of candy bars, and some ice cream.

I saw food as an outlet. It was like a drug to me. Whenever I was depressed or angry, I would eat. When I was happy, I would celebrate...and eat. I realized that what I

was doing wasn't quite right, but I didn't have the strength to stop. Food was my escape. When I first started throwing up, I weighed 120 pounds and I had 10% body fat. I had never been fat. It was all in my mind. At the end, I weighed about 100 pounds and had just 3% body fat. Professional athletes have 6 to 10% body fat.

Emotionally, I wasn't very stable. Probably that's where the eating thing came from. My mom was an alcoholic and there was nothing I could do about it. Her mom had also been an alcoholic and she had been severely abused so she didn't know what it took to be a good mother. My mom and I had never really been close. I kept everything to myself and I couldn't express anger or sadness or even excitement. I dealt with my feelings by eating.

My mom started to notice that I was throwing up and confronted me about it. All I could do was cry. I tried to stop throwing up. It worked for about a day. After that, I just got a lot better at hiding my habit. After I had been bulimic for about 2 years, I was looking really bad. I had no energy in my body. I fell asleep in class all the time. I never did homework, and I didn't have the energy to be with my friends in my last year in high school.

At home, things were starting to get pretty bad. My dad had moved for his job and my mom and I were constantly fighting. She would deal with her problems by drinking more and I knew that I could no longer live with her and survive. I told my mom that I was moving and I couldn't see her anymore while she was drinking.

I got my own apartment and graduated from high school. Suddenly, I was all on my own. That's when I decided that things were going to change. I was only going to concentrate on me. I wanted to be able to feel good about myself. I started researching about bulimia and anorexia. What I found was shocking. I never realized the extent of damage I had been doing to my body. I had a complete medical check-up, and my condition was scary. I had all my teeth checked out and repaired. The acid in your stomach ruins your teeth and since I was throwing up quite a bit, it was pretty bad.

I began to help myself. I changed my eating habits. I never went shopping on an empty stomach, and I could only buy enough food for 1 meal. Instead of having 3 meals a day, I had 5 small ones. In between meals, I would try to keep myself busy so I wouldn't think about food all the time. It took about 6 months before I could sit down and read a book without needing food.

In addition, I took a year out of my life to take care of myself and work on the problems that caused the bulimia in the first place. It was a lot of hard work but definitely worth it. I would never encourage anybody to try to get over an eating disorder without help. For me, it was almost a full time job to be able to take care of myself. I am very lucky that I had friends that were supportive enough to help me out whenever they could.

I am now able to look in the mirror and like what I see. That's the key. I learned how to like myself no matter what I imagine I see in the mirror. I realized I had been seeing something in the mirror that wasn't there...probably what I felt like, not what I looked like. It can still be hard sometimes. They say bulimia is never 100% curable, but I know that I'll never make myself throw up again. Yet, sometimes I still worry too much about what I'm eating, but now, at least, I know how to deal with it.

I see a lot of people who have the same problems I had. In fact, 20% of college women have tried bulimia. They just don't realize how serious it can get. It's a progressive condition. I try to help people before it gets too late and I hope some people can use my knowledge and experience to get better.

Michael's Story

Childhood for me in Charleston, South Carolina was great. I never starved and never worried about clothing or bathing thanks to Mama. My mother is a fascinating lady. Mama brought our family pride and respect. Raising 4 kids was not an easy task. My dad was around and we did things together but he lived elsewhere. Still, my upbringing was very positive. I never, ever had problems with the law or drugs as a child even though drugs and crime were around. Part of this was due to Mama, part due to the neighbors in the 'hood' who were always positive and encouraging towards me. Charleston was segregated and we lived in our part of the town and in the 70's, the world was troubled with racism as it is today but as small children, we were protected from much of the ugliness. (Even today, in spite of problems, my neighborhood is still

strong.) I was given love and support which protected me for many years but my problems with substances came later in life.

My life was directed toward sports such as football and track. Sports was a way out of poverty. It was hard to get a job that you felt really good about. I played sports through Pop Warner and college. I received numerous awards and honors from high school and through 2 colleges.

Then I became aware of a world different from where I grew up in. After a year at a local college in Charleston, I went to a Midwest college. I played football there but my life dream was to play professional football. But getting cut in the last round of tryouts by the Packers shattered my world. I felt that I failed a lot of people who expected me to play professional football on TV.

Most of all, I felt like a failure. My self-esteem was at an all-time low. My whole life, I felt, was sports. I felt I needed to fit in, to be with the social crowd in the college town in Iowa where I settled. Sometimes it was wonderful, going out and being sociable, but yet, I felt so lost in a predominantly white culture. All of a sudden, I didn't think too highly of myself. I started hanging out with a crowd that used grass and coke. I guess you can say peer pressure helped cause me to become a lost soul.

Also, it seemed impossible to get a job. So I started doing drugs for recreation which quickly turned to abuse. I was getting so out of it, I scared myself. I was out of control, even selling a little to friends to support my use. The drug was controlling me. And I felt helpless, I felt spineless, and a few other disgusting names. The lady I loved was afraid of me and we separated. My world was starting to crumble. I had one last chance and that was to tell my mother about my behavior. The lady I respected, the lady I loved, I was about to tell her how disturbed I was. Sadness hit me as soon as I spoke about my problem over the phone. My mother was very hurt, making the statement, 'I didn't bring you up that way.' My mother's advice was pray first, love yourself and respect yourself and everything will happen good for you.

As I looked in the mirror after talking to my mother on the phone, I said, 'Enough. Never again will I look like that . . . eyes all glassy, unshaven for days.'

You get the picture. The key words were to pray to God, love yourself, and most of all, respect yourself. Being homeless and hitting rock bottom was no fun. But thanks to the strength my Mama gave me and to my lovely lady and sons that I helped raise, I gave them a better picture to look at. It's been 9 years since I had drugs in my body. Never again. No one should go through the drug route.

It takes a strong individual to survive the temptation of drugs. I learned lessons the hard way. Support from my family and friends pulled me out of the pits with kindness and love, and today I'm happy to say I'm alive, mentally and physically. Presently I'm managing a sporting goods store in Iowa, I'm still very active in sports and I still am with my nice, soothing lady for 13 years, and I try to give to my kids what my Mama gave me.

CHAPTER 26

Double Trouble
Mental/Emotional Problems And Drugs

Acknowledging the connection between mental, emotional, and substance abuse problems makes it possible to prevent their escalation and lessen their severity.

One of the reasons people do unusual things when they have a temporary emotional crisis or suffer from mental illness is that their brain chemistry is unbalanced. One of the reasons people do unusual things when they use psychoactive drugs is that drugs unbalance their brain chemistry. In fact, since many of the same brain chemicals are involved, the symptoms of almost any emotional crisis or mental illness can resemble symptoms induced by psychoactive drugs or withdrawal from them. For example:

- Cocaine abuse can mimic paranoia.

- Alcohol abuse or amphetamine withdrawal can imitate major depression.

  Conversely, people with certain mental problems look like they use drugs.

- Someone with a major depression might seem to be using Valium or alcohol.

- A person suffering from schizophrenia can act like someone on LSD.

- Someone smoking marijuana can seem to have attention deficit disorder (ADD).

Some people suffering emotional crises or from mental illness often try to self-medicate with illegal or legal psychoactive drugs to try to rebalance their brain chemistry. A person who experiences bouts of depression, for example, might be drawn to cocaine or another stimulant to try to elevate his or her mood. Someone else who is extremely anxious or irritable might be drawn to alcohol, a sedative like Halcion, or heroin.

❝ "I'd been depressed a lot before trying amphetamines and somehow, getting wired worked for a while. It lifted the depression, but then when I crashed, I was twice as depressed and that was when I tried out my suicidal thoughts."

19-year-old college sophomore

FYI When mental or emotional difficulties become prolonged and incapacitating, there are a number of alternatives to self-medication.

- **Self-help groups** (Emotions Anonymous, Double Trouble — 12-step group for mentally ill substance abusers, etc.);
- **Group therapy** (facilitated by a therapist);
- **Psychotherapy** (individual sessions with a therapist);
- **Psychiatric medication** (prescribed by a physician or psychiatrist).

Workbook Exercise 1: Throughout life, people have mental and emotional symptoms that they may think are signs of mental illness, but most mental or emotional difficulties are short-term. Some use their own methods to control their feelings and thoughts. List several positive non-drug alternatives people can use to calm themselves if they feel anxious, lift their spirits if they feel depressed, and cool themselves off if they are angry.

EXERCISE

1

Anxiety: _____

_____

_____

Depression: _____

_____

_____

Anger: _____

_____

_____

❝ "When I went to college, it was the first time I was away from home. I was very unhappy. I tried drinking beer, but that only made me more depressed. I drank endless cups of coffee, but that only made me nervous and still depressed. Finally, a friend suggested I join a group just to meet people, so I joined, of all things, a square dance group. It ended my isolation and by the end of the year, I felt much more confident, happier, and my depression never returned. The exercise I got by dancing didn't hurt either."

College grad

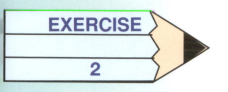

EXERCISE

2

Workbook Exercise 2: One of the signs that a person may be having problems (mental, emotional, or drug related) is isolation. Shyness could be a contributing factor, so could weak social skills. List 5 ways to help a friend be less isolated (e.g., ask a classmate to go out to lunch).

1) _____

_____

2) _____

_____

3) _____

_____

4) _____

_____

5) _____

_____

FYI It is helpful to know the difference between having temporary emotional and mental difficulties and having a chronic mental or emotional illness that disrupts one's life, even though either problem can cause a person to self-medicate. Some of the major mental illnesses are

- **Major depression** (clinical depression): depressed mood, diminished interest and pleasure, sleep and appetite disturbances, and feelings of worthlessness that last for more than 2 weeks;
- **Manic-depression:** alternating periods of major depression, normalcy, and mania (a persistantly elevated and agitated mood);
- **Schizophrenia:** thought disorder, believed to be mostly inherited, characterized by hallucinations, delusions, poor idea association, inappropriate emotions;
- **Anxiety disorders:** series of disorders that can include muscle tension, restlessness, stomach irritation, sweating, heart palpitations, hyper-vigilance, excessive worry, difficulty concentrating, shortness of breath;
- **Antisocial personality disorder:** disorder in which the person is impulsive, aggressive, irresponsible, prone to alcohol and drug abuse, sexually promiscuous, apt to engage in criminal activities, and apt to have difficulty with self-control.

Most kinds of drug addiction, including alcoholism, are listed by the American Psychiatric Association as forms of mental illness.

Group Exercise 1: Since the use of drugs can magnify a person's depression (whether it is short-term or long-term), it is important to be aware of the problem and how to help. Have someone who works the suicide or crisis hotline or an on-campus counselor talk to the class about the signs they listen for to decide whether someone is deeply depressed or suicidal, and some of the things they say or do to help them. Then discuss some of the ways members of the group could help a friend who is deeply depressed.

> ❝ "I tell members of my family that I'm in a half-way house for drug addiction as opposed to a mental health half-way house because it seems, in their eyes, with drug addiction I can get better, but with mental illness, they see it as a chronic problem. There's a stigma."
>
> 19-year-old with major depression

Group Exercise 2: Have the class discuss the stigma of mental illness. Consider such things as

- Do people talk about it at all, even if someone they know is affected?
- Even though the problems are often connected, is drug abuse more socially acceptable than mental illness?
- How does the media portray mental illness?

FYI In a 1990 study by the National Institute of Mental Health, 53% of those who abuse drugs and 37% of those who abuse alcohol had, in addition to their drug problem, at least 1 serious mental illness. Conversely, 29% of people with mental illness had a problem with either alcohol or other drug use. The overlap is greater with certain drugs: 76% of those who abuse cocaine and 50% of those who abuse marijuana had a diagnosable mental disorder. The most common disorders are major depression, manic-depression, schizophrenia, antisocial personality disorder, and some form of anxiety.

PI **Personal Inquiry:** Write about a time when you felt depressed or anxious for more than a week. What did you feel and what did you do to counteract those feelings?

With A Little Help From My Friends

Groups, Mentors, And Role Models

This chapter examines the advantages of working with others for your mutual benefit as well as the value of using mentors and role models.

No matter who you are, no matter what desires you have, no matter what problems you battle, there are others feeling similar things, handling similar problems, or involved in similar kinds of relationships. So, when you have a problem to solve, a difficult task to complete, or simply need someone to talk to, there's almost always someone else or some group that has experienced a similar thing and probably found an answer that you could use. Those people could be peers, mentors, or role models. We will use the following definition:

Peers are people that have something in common: e.g., common behaviors, interests, goals, values, or problems.
Mentors are people whose advice or help one can count on. They are usually older.
Role models are people whom one admires and wishes to imitate.

There are formal and informal ways to work with peers. Informal ways include talking with a friend you've come to trust, asking advice of a person who's worked through the same problems as you, or even getting together with several people who have similar interests, as in a study group.

A more formal way to work with peers is to join a self-help group such as Alcoholics Anonymous, Gamblers Anonymous, or Alanon (people who live with alcoholics). There are also peer counseling groups where students help other students work on common interests, goals, and problems. There are associations of people with similar interests such as an Hispanic-American cultural group, a church group, a social service organization, or one of the dozens of support groups that can be found listed in the local newspaper or phone book.

In working with peers, 3 steps are needed: present the problem, find a solution, and act on the solution. The relationship with a mentor is more long-term and often crucial to growth. A mentor can be a relative, teacher, upper classmate, or other older person you trust, who can guide or support you through dozens of decisions you need to make. A role model can be someone you know, someone you work with, someone you have heard or read about, or someone in the media.

Workbook Exercise 1: It is helpful to know whom you would go to if you needed advice, help with a problem, or just someone who would listen. Note 1 or 2 qualities you would look for in a peer or mentor whom you could talk to or who would advise you on the following problem areas:

1) Relationship or sexual matters: _____

_____

_____

2) Emotional matters (e.g., loneliness, fear, desire): _____

_____

_____

3) Spiritual matters: _____

_____

_____

4) Financial or legal matters: _____

_____

_____

5) Educational (help with major or studying): _____

_____

_____

6) Work (what direction you should take on the job) or career decisions: _____

_____

_____

7) Problem with a substance such as alcohol or another drug: _____

_____

_____

_____

Workbook Exercise 2: Name 3 public figures you would like to use or have used as role models.

EXERCISE 2

1) _____

2) _____

3) _____

EXERCISE 3

Workbook Exercise 3: Summarize 3 benefits you have received working in small groups while using this workbook e.g., being able to learn with others rather than feeling I have to do it all by myself.

1) _____

_____

_____

2) _____

_____

_____

3) _____

_____

_____

EXERCISE 4

Workbook Exercise 4: Summarize an experience you had that you could share with others that might give them insight into a similar problem. For example, if you had difficulty getting up and talking in front of a group, tell what you did to overcome your fears, or if you had a fight with your parents, what actions you took to become reconciled.

_____

_____

_____

_____

_____

_____

_____

_____

_____

_____

_____

_____

GROUP EXERCISE

Group Exercise 1: In any group, there is a very large amount of collective knowledge that can be called on. Have the group write questions on cards that they would like answered. Collect the cards and have 1 or 2 "readers" select appropriate questions and offer them to the group as a whole for a solution or answer. The questions can be on any subject.

Group Exercise 2: Discuss the differences between working by yourself, working in small groups, or working in large groups. Make reference to your own experiences in using this workbook.

> " "I always hated to ask for help. I would get lost rather than ask for directions. I thought asking for help was a sign of weakness. But one day a friend took me to a self-help Alanon meeting for people who have an alcoholic in their family. A woman, 10 years older, started telling about her problems with her husband who drank. She wasn't anything like me I thought, but her story was mine. We were soul-mates by virtue of having the same problem. She started telling what she had done to solve her problems and I thought, 'I can do that.' And I did."
>
> 23-year-old male member of Alanon

Personal Inquiry: Write about someone who has been a mentor or role model for you. Describe how her or his example, advice, or concern has made a difference in your life.

CHAPTER 28

Help! I Need Somebody
Finding and Using Support Services

Knowing what resources are available in your community before they are needed can prevent physical and psychological trauma and even save lives.

9-1-1

If you have ever been in an emergency situation, you know that time is a critical factor. Even if it's not an emergency, knowing where to go for help will make you more confident and effective. Knowledge of what services are available in the community and how to access them before you need them could make you calm and decisive during a chaotic situation.

Most situations are not emergencies but chronic problems which erode an individual's ability to keep in psychological or physical balance. The following services can help people in crises or help them to manage deep-seated, continuing problems.

Support services are listed in your telephone directory. The basic categories of help and some representative examples are as follows:

Emergency
- **Physical emergencies:** 911, fire, police, hospital emergency room, poison control;
- **Mental/emotional emergencies:** suicide prevention, battered women's center, crisis intervention.

Non-Emergency
- **Medical care:** hospital, local physician, student health clinic, county health department;
- **Drug/alcohol treatment facilities:** county drug and alcohol department, in-patient, out-patient;
- **Mental health:** county department of mental health, private in- and out-patient facilities;
- **General counseling:** student counseling center, rape/violence counseling, private practitioners;
- **Self-help groups:** Alcoholics Anonymous (AA), Narcotics Anonymous (NA), Adult Children of Alcoholics (Alcoa, Alanon, AlaTeen, Gamblers Anonymous (GA);
- **Financial aid:** county general assistance program, credit counseling, student counseling.

If people think they are having a crisis, treat it seriously rather than try to talk them out of it. While intoxicated, people might feel that they are in a life-threatening situation, and even if they aren't, respect the fact that they are experiencing a psychological crisis. When in doubt and particularly when you suspect a crisis that suggests immediate harm will occur, **CALL 911.**

Workbook Exercise 1: Research 7 of the individual services found on the first page of this chapter that you think you might one day need (e.g., student counseling center). Enter the name, phone number, address, hours, services, and other pertinent details. Because this information should be available to you, make a copy of this sheet and keep it handy.

1) _____
_____
_____
_____

2) _____
_____
_____
_____

3) _____
_____
_____
_____

4) _____
_____
_____
_____

5) _____
_____
_____
_____

6) _____
_____
_____
_____

7) _____
_____
_____
_____

EXCELLENCE IN HEALTH CARE
24 HOUR EMERGENCY SERVICE

Workbook Exercise 2: Individually or in pairs, interview a support service professional such as an emergency room nurse or visit a 12-step support group meeting (AA, NA, OA, etc.). Write up a report in which you include the contact person's name, services available, and a summary of the interview/visit. (If you visit a support group, summarize your impression of the kind of help offered, the way to join the group, etc., but respect confidentiality.)

Crisis Intervention Service

_____

_____

_____

_____

_____

_____

_____

_____

_____

_____

_____

_____

_____

_____

_____

Workbook Exercise 3: Summarize a situation you experienced where someone was going through a crisis and you either acted to help the person or weren't quite sure what you should do (e.g., a friend who sounded suicidal and you told him to talk to his minister). Knowing what you do now, what other options would you have?

A NIGHTTIME MINISTRY
FOR THOSE IN CRISIS
Available 7 Nights A Week
HOURS: 10PM-4AM

_____

_____

_____

_____

_____

_____

_____

_____

_____

_____

_____

_____

_____

_____

GROUP EXERCISE

Group Exercise 1: Divide the group into teams and have each team make an in-depth investigation of 1 of the categories below. Each group should end up with a list of programs in that category with pertinent details and information on them. Be as specific as possible Then have each group deliver a 5-minute report to the class on their category.

- Emergency physical services
- Emergency mental/emotional services
- Non-emergency medical care
- Drug/alcohol treatment services
- Mental health treatment services
- General counseling services
- Self-help groups
- Financial and career counseling

FYI There are over 20,000 reported accidental deaths from drug interactions or overdoses per year and over 463,000 emergency room visits where drugs (other than alcohol) were mentioned as a cause. The actual numbers are thought to be much higher.

Group Exercise 2: Invite an emergency room doctor, intern, or nurse to your class and have him or her speak about the frequency and variety of alcohol and other drug-related problems.

Personal Inquiry: Which of the services that you have discovered in this chapter most answers a need that you, a friend, or a family member has? What practical steps would it take to get you or another person to those services?

Do Not Pass Go! Do Not Collect $200!

The Costs Of Use

Compulsive behavior, particularly with alcohol and drugs, is expensive. Awareness of the actual costs in lost dollars, lost time, and lost freedom makes avoidance of drug abuse easier.

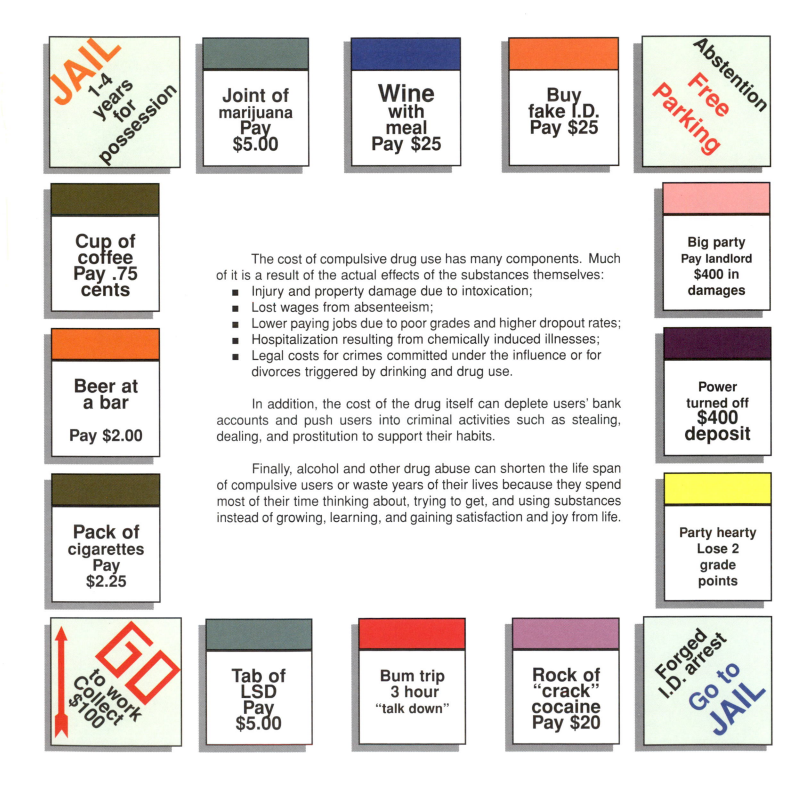

JAIL 1-4 years for possession

Joint of marijuana Pay $5.00

Wine with meal Pay $25

Buy fake I.D. Pay $25

Abstention Free Parking

Cup of coffee Pay .75 cents

Big party Pay landlord $400 in damages

The cost of compulsive drug use has many components. Much of it is a result of the actual effects of the substances themselves:

- Injury and property damage due to intoxication;
- Lost wages from absenteeism;
- Lower paying jobs due to poor grades and higher dropout rates;
- Hospitalization resulting from chemically induced illnesses;
- Legal costs for crimes committed under the influence or for divorces triggered by drinking and drug use.

In addition, the cost of the drug itself can deplete users' bank accounts and push users into criminal activities such as stealing, dealing, and prostitution to support their habits.

Finally, alcohol and other drug abuse can shorten the life span of compulsive users or waste years of their lives because they spend most of their time thinking about, trying to get, and using substances instead of growing, learning, and gaining satisfaction and joy from life.

Beer at a bar Pay $2.00

Power turned off $400 deposit

Pack of cigarettes Pay $2.25

Party hearty Lose 2 grade points

GO to work Collect $100

Tab of LSD Pay $5.00

Bum trip 3 hour "talk down"

Rock of "crack" cocaine Pay $20

Forged I.D. arrest Go to JAIL

Workbook Exercise 1: Calculate what different levels of drinking cost. (One drink means 12 oz. of beer, 5 oz. of wine, 1 1/2 oz. of hard liquor alone or in a mixed drink, or 1 1/2 oz. of a liqueur.)

EXERCISE 1

	6 drinks per week	20 drinks per week
Kind of drink: _____		
Cost per week:	_____	_____
Cost per month:	_____	_____
Cost per year:	_____	_____
Cost for 4 years:	_____	_____
	Per Week	Per Year
Hours spent drinking or getting alcohol:	_____	_____

Don't pay taxes
Go back 3 spaces

Dubious friend borrows money
Lose **$100**

Workbook Exercise 2: Without consideration of the health risks, calculate the cost of a pack-a-day habit over a 4 year period.

EXERCISE 2

	Per month	Per year	4 years
Brand: _____			
Cost of the cigarettes:	_____	_____	_____

1 gram of cocaine
Pay **$100**

Unprotected sex
$75 for antibiotic

Run out of money
Take a chance

Max out credit cards
Take 2nd part-time job

1 ounce sinsemilla
Pay **$250**

Win
drinking contest
Scholastic probation

Friend hurls on rug
$50 to carpet cleaner

Workbook Exercise 3: Find out the financial cost of a drunk driving arrest in your locale assuming there are no injuries, property damage, or loss of life.

Attorney's fees: _____

Fines: _____

Legal costs: _____

Increase in auto insurance rates: _____

Increase in health insurance rates: _____

List 3 ways a DUI conviction could damage future job prospects.

1) _____

2) _____

3) _____

Friend in "rhoid rage"
$700 for new furniture

Hangovers
Miss 25 work days
Lose $2,500

Workbook Exercise 4: A cocaine habit frequently starts with a weekend binge. It often turns into a weekly and even a daily ritual. One gram of coke costs $100 and will supply about 10 doses (lines). The major effects from a line of cocaine will last 30-45 minutes, but the drug is extremely compulsive and can be used several times in an evening. Calculate the cost of

	One Month	One Year
1/2 gram per week:	_____	_____
1 gram per week:	_____	_____
4 grams per week:	_____	_____

List 3 things you could buy in 1 year with the money spent on 1 gram per week.

1) _____

2) _____

3) _____

"Druggie" friend moves in
Evicted

Take up gambling
Lose paycheck

Cocaine binging
10 rocks per weekend
Pay $9,000/yr

Hungry slot machine
Car repossessed

Heavy drinking
$6,500 a year

Holdup
No money, no stash, no friends

Roll car
5 days in traction
Pay $10,000

Fired from work
Go to
AA
meeting

Give up smoking
Gain 6 years of life

Overdose
Game over

Sell to narc!
Uh oh!
Go to jail

Deal "pot" to friends to pay for your own. Worry.

DUI conviction
$5,000 court costs

Bankruptcy
Pay
everything

Group Exercise 1: Invite someone within the criminal justice system or a professor of criminology to speak about alcohol and drug-related crimes. With his or her help, discuss local and state laws regarding the use of illegal drugs. Find out the penalties for possession and dealing marijuana, cocaine, and LSD.

Alcohol is also a drug which is usually a co-factor in many types of crimes including I.D. card forgery, public intoxication, vandalism, and simple assault. Find out what the penalties are for these offenses.

 The cost of maintaining 1 prisoner in the California Department of Corrections is $20,760. Currently 43,034 people are in California state prisons for drug related offenses, another 3,012 are in the system for DUI's, while 22,000 are on parole. Incarceration plus the cost of supervising parolees exceeds $1 billion a year.

In Massachusetts, the cost per prisoner is over $32,000 which is the equivalent of tuition and living expenses at Harvard for 1 year.

Group Exercise 2: Pick a small group of students to go to the local court when arraignments and pleas are taken. Observe the people who are arraigned for drug crimes. Then give a report to the class on what you saw.

 Over 7% of all 1991 college freshman (120,000) in the U.S. became drop-outs for alcohol-related reasons. They will lose $33 billion in lifetime earnings.
- Drug users are absent from work twice as often as non-using company employees.
- Drug users incur medical costs that average 3 times higher than non-using company employees.
- Drug users are 5 times as likely to be involved in accidents when off the job.
- Each employee with a drug or alcohol problem costs a company an average of $5,000 a year.

The estimated loss to the national economy from drug and alcohol problems for 1 year is more than $150 billion.

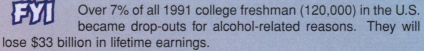 **Personal Inquiry:** If you drink, discuss whether the cost in money and lost time, or the possibility of arrest has ever been a factor in your use of alcohol. If you don't drink, discuss how another's drinking might cost you money and time.

Graduate in 4 years
3 job offers

Avoid DUI arrest
Save year's tuition

2 years clean and sober
Save $13,000

No drug/alcohol problems
Lifetime earnings up by $350,000

Never used
Never will

Been There, Done That
Where Do I Go From Here?

By reflecting on what you have accomplished through the use of this workbook,
you will be able to affirm your strengths and decide
how you can use them.

A MATTER OF BALANCE has emphasized that although psychoactive substances produce beneficial, desirable, and pleasurable effects, there is a cost. If we then choose to use alcohol or other drugs, we are vulnerable to the negative consequences. Our vulnerability depends on our genetic makeup, internal and external pressures to abuse drugs, and the addictive potential of the drugs themselves. If we feel we are vulnerable, there are protective measures we can take to avoid having to rely on drugs for their benefits and to reduce the harmful consequences if we do use psychoactive substances. Finally, there are resources available to help people who have unhealthy relationships with alcohol and other drugs.

In using this workbook and having had a chance to discuss issues or compare experiences with class members, you may have discovered illuminating facts about substances and human behavior as well as their interconnections. You may have also clarified your own values and discovered different perspectives on alcohol and other drug issues. Hopefully, practicing new skills and activities has strengthened your own good habits and diminished or eliminated any unhealthy ones you might have.

NAME ______________________ DATE ___/___/___

Exercises Chapter 30

EXERCISE 1

Workbook Exercise 1: Take a few minutes to review the previous 29 chapters of your workbook. Summarize specific things in 5 chapters that have been the most useful, relevant, and valuable for you.

1) ______________________

2) ______________________

3) ______________________

4) ______________________

5) ______________________

EXERCISE 2

Workbook Exercise 2: What do you think you will you remember from your experiences with the workbook long after the class is over?

____

EXERCISE 3

Workbook Exercise 3: Three questions you still have about substance use issues are

1) ______________________

2) ______________________

3) ______________________

Workbook Exercise 4: Action Plans: Summarize what activities you could undertake that would be helpful to you, your friends, family, school, workplace, or your community. Think about building on strengths as well as working on any problems that might exist.

Example:
Present situation: On Hump Day [Wednesday], people in my residence hall start noisy partying and it goes on into the next morning.

Goal: I'd like the dorm to be a quieter place, especially during the week.

Action necessary: Start speaking privately to my friends about the spillover effect of partying ("second-hand drinking").

1) Yourself:

   Present situation: _____

   _____

   Goal: _____

   _____

   Action necessary: _____

   _____

2) Friend/relative:

   Present situation: _____

   _____

   Goal: _____

   _____

   Action necessary: _____

   _____

3) School/workplace/community:

   Present situation: _____

   _____

   Goal: _____

   _____

   Action necessary: _____

   _____

Getting high naturally

Group Exercise 1: To the Wall (Again)

To find out how knowledge and attitudes have changed during your course, have members of the class repeat the Group Exercise in Chapter 1 in which they wrote down their ideas, feelings, and experiences about alcohol, tobacco, and other drugs. Use whichever format you used for the Chapter 1 version of this exercise (either butcher paper taped to the wall or paper or cards taped to the wall).

Afterwards, have the entire class read the results and discuss what has been written. Some ideas to consider are

- the most typical response;
- unusual or memorable responses;
- the different kinds of responses;
- strikingly contrasting responses.

(Afterwards, time permitting, if the original "wall exercise" is still available, it can be put up, and the differences between the first and second version can then be discussed by the group.)

Group Exercise 2: You have written about yourself extensively in the **Personal Inquiries**. These writing episodes have been designed to let you explore your own ideas, feelings, values, and problems. In small groups, discuss whether the process of writing about yourself and these subjects has been valuable. Is it a tool that you might use in the future? What have you actually gotten out of the process of writing about yourself?

Personal
Inquiries

Personal Inquiry
Chapter 1

Discuss the kinds of drug education you have received and discuss whether it has had an impact on you.

_____

_____

_____

_____

_____

_____

_____

_____

_____

_____

_____

_____

_____

_____

_____

_____

_____

_____

_____

_____

_____

_____

_____

Think of the last 3 times you were drinking or with someone who was drinking. For each time, discuss whether the anticipated outcome was the actual outcome.

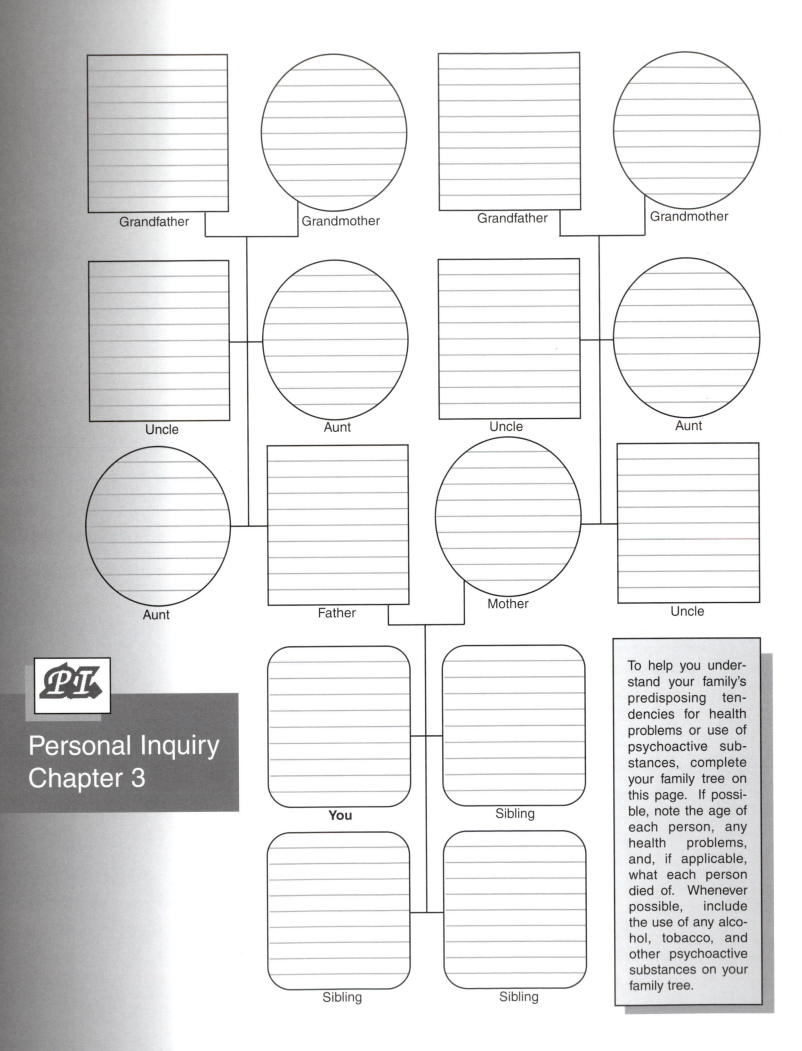

Grandfather

Grandmother

Grandfather

Grandmother

Uncle

Aunt

Uncle

Aunt

Aunt

Father

Mother

Uncle

Personal Inquiry Chapter 3

You

Sibling

Sibling

Sibling

To help you understand your family's predisposing tendencies for health problems or use of psychoactive substances, complete your family tree on this page. If possible, note the age of each person, any health problems, and, if applicable, what each person died of. Whenever possible, include the use of any alcohol, tobacco, and other psychoactive substances on your family tree.

Write about 3 stressors from your early environment that you do or would handle differently now. For example, you used to respond to your parents yelling at you by getting out of the house. Now you are willing to face the confrontation and try to resolve the issues.

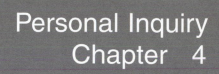

Personal Inquiry
Chapter 4

_____

_____

_____

_____

_____

_____

_____

_____

_____

_____

_____

_____

_____

_____

_____

_____

_____

_____

_____

_____

_____

_____

_____

_____

Personal Inquiry
Chapter 5

Discuss a time when using a substance or doing something either threatened to become compulsive or became compulsive and was causing you some harm (e.g., watching T.V., playing pool). What did you do or could you have done to break the pattern of use or activity?

Summarize a natural high you have had. Include what led up to it, the setting, the experience itself, and how you value it now.

Personal Inquiry
Chapter 7

Given the state of your physical health, note any areas that you might want to improve.

_____
_____
_____
_____
_____
_____
_____
_____
_____
_____
_____
_____
_____
_____
_____
_____
_____
_____
_____
_____
_____
_____
_____
_____
_____
_____
_____

Discuss which aspects of your wellness (physical, intellectual, emotional, spiritual, or social) are most responsible for your decision not to use or overuse psychoactive substances.

Personal Inquiry
Chapter 9

If you were to die tomorrow what would your epitaph be? If you were to die at the age of 70, what do you hope your epitaph would be?

_____

_____

_____

_____

_____

_____

_____

_____

_____

_____

_____

_____

_____

_____

_____

_____

_____

_____

_____

_____

_____

_____

Make a contract with yourself to change some area of your life that you wish to strengthen.

PERSONAL CHANGE CONTRACT

I,_____ (*your name*), on _____ (*today's date*), agree to change, strengthen, or begin to do the following:

_____

_____ I will share this commitment with

_____

(*name of person(s)*) and by_____ (*future date*), I will report back to the above person(s) about the outcome of this agreement and my ideas and feelings about my experiences.

Signed _____

Plan of Action: _____

_____

_____

_____

_____

_____

_____

_____

_____

_____

_____

_____

_____

_____

_____

_____

_____

_____

_____

_____

_____

Personal Inquiry
Chapter 11

Write about something you have done that you didn't feel good about but went ahead and did anyway because you thought most people were doing it (e.g., heavy drinking, sex, etc.).

_____
_____
_____
_____
_____
_____
_____
_____
_____
_____
_____
_____
_____
_____
_____
_____
_____
_____
_____
_____
_____
_____
_____

Answers to selected questions in Normative Assessment Survey

6) C. 45%   8) C. 11-20%   9) D. 15-17%   13) B. 15%   14) C. 80%
16) E. 90%   17) 10-15%   18) E. 80-90%   19) B. 30-35%

Based on your cultural values and what you have seen so far, what traditions would you pass on to your children regarding alcohol and other drug use?

Personal Inquiry
Chapter 12

_____

_____

_____

_____

_____

_____

_____

_____

_____

_____

_____

_____

_____

_____

_____

_____

_____

_____

_____

_____

_____

_____

_____

_____

_____

Personal Inquiry
Chapter 13

Describe how much and in what ways you might have been influenced by music, music videos, and other media portrayals of the following:

How you display sexual interest in another person;
How you have defined your attitude and "look."

_____

_____

_____

_____

_____

_____

_____

_____

_____

_____

_____

_____

_____

_____

_____

_____

_____

_____

_____

_____

Write an account of a friend's or your own tobacco history including why the first cigarette was smoked or the first chew taken, what level of use was reached, and whether there was a desire or attempt to stop. If attempts were made, how many were there, and if the final attempt was successful, how was it accomplished?

Personal Inquiry
Chapter 15

Which responsibilities of adulthood are you looking forward to and which ones would you rather not have to deal with?

_____

_____

_____

_____

_____

_____

_____

_____

_____

_____

_____

_____

_____

_____

_____

_____

_____

_____

_____

_____

_____

_____

_____

_____

Rate yourself on how often you use the following social skills:

	Often	Sometimes	Never
Initiate conversations	___	___	___
Carry on conversations	___	___	___
Give compliments	___	___	___
Receive compliments	___	___	___
Express an emotion	___	___	___
Refuse an unreasonable request	___	___	___
Ask a stranger a question	___	___	___

Write about 2 skills that you consider your strengths.

_____

_____

_____

_____

_____

_____

_____

_____

_____

_____

_____

_____

_____

_____

_____

_____

_____

_____

_____

_____

_____

_____

_____

_____

Personal Inquiry
Chapter 17

Describe ways to be sexually intimate or physically affectionate without having sexual intercourse or an exchange of body fluids.

_____
_____
_____
_____
_____
_____
_____
_____
_____
_____
_____
_____
_____
_____
_____
_____
_____
_____
_____
_____
_____
_____
_____
_____

Have you ever lost control, assaulted someone, or been assaulted during or after drinking, or witnessed such an assault? Thinking over the experience now, what could have been done to avoid or lessen the harm done?

_____
_____
_____
_____
_____
_____
_____
_____
_____
_____
_____
_____
_____
_____
_____
_____
_____
_____
_____
_____
_____
_____
_____
_____

Personal Inquiry
Chapter 19

Describe an occasion when good harm-reduction planning saved you from grief (or could have).

_____

_____

_____

_____

_____

_____

_____

_____

_____

_____

_____

_____

_____

_____

_____

_____

_____

_____

_____

_____

_____

_____

_____

_____

_____

_____

_____

_____

_____

_____

Give the reasons why you would or wouldn't want to be involved with campus or community activities that might improve your school and neighborhood in relation to alcohol and drug problems. Discuss whether you think these kinds of activities make a difference.

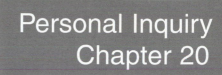

Personal Inquiry
Chapter 20

Personal Inquiry
Chapter 21

Describe a friend or relative you saw going through problems with drug or alcohol use. Based on what you now know, what actions would you take?

_____
_____
_____
_____
_____
_____
_____
_____
_____
_____
_____
_____
_____
_____
_____
_____
_____
_____
_____
_____
_____
_____
_____
_____
_____
_____
_____

List past attitudes or activities which you had difficulty admitting harmed you (e.g., drinking or "front-loading" before you went to a party and getting very drunk). What kept you from admitting it and why? Next to that list, note what you did or could have done to change those behaviors

Personal Inquiry
Chapter 23

Summarize a difficult ethical decision you made concerning alcohol/drug use that involved enabling. Discuss whether you are satisfied with the outcome, and whether you might now make a different decision.

_____
_____
_____
_____
_____
_____
_____
_____
_____
_____
_____
_____
_____
_____
_____
_____
_____
_____
_____
_____
_____
_____
_____
_____
_____
_____

Discuss whether you personally are most susceptible to direct pressure, indirect pressure, or self-imposed pressure to use psychoactive drugs or engage in sex.

_____
_____
_____
_____
_____
_____
_____
_____
_____
_____
_____
_____
_____
_____
_____
_____
_____
_____
_____
_____
_____
_____
_____
_____

Personal Inquiry
Chapter 25

Note any particular foods (e.g., chocolate, pasta, doughnuts) or eating behaviors (e.g., "I can refuse one piece of my binge food, I can't refuse the second.") which have affected you physically, mentally, or emotionally. If there are such foods or behaviors, write down 1 beginning step to change (e.g., making sure none of that binge food is in your apartment or dorm).

_____
_____
_____
_____
_____
_____
_____
_____
_____
_____
_____
_____
_____
_____
_____
_____
_____
_____
_____
_____

Write about a time when you felt depressed or anxious for more than a week. What did you feel and what did you do to counteract those feelings?

Personal Inquiry
Chapter 27

Write about someone who has been a mentor or role model for you. Describe how her or his example, advice, or concern has made a difference in your life.

_____
_____
_____
_____
_____
_____
_____
_____
_____
_____
_____
_____
_____
_____
_____
_____
_____
_____
_____
_____
_____
_____
_____
_____
_____

Which of the services that you have discovered in this chapter most answers a need that you, a friend, or a family member has? What practical steps would it take to get you or another person to those services?

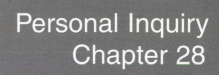

_____
_____
_____
_____
_____
_____
_____
_____
_____
_____
_____
_____
_____
_____
_____
_____
_____
_____
_____
_____
_____
_____
_____

Personal Inquiry
Chapter 29

If you drink, discuss whether the cost in money and lost time, or the possibility of arrest has ever been a factor in your use of alcohol. Also discuss what expense in dollars or legal difficulties would influence you to reduce your intake.

_____

_____

_____

_____

_____

_____

_____

_____

_____

_____

_____

_____

_____

_____

_____

_____

_____

_____

_____

_____

_____

_____

_____

_____

_____

_____

_____

BIBLIOGRAPHY

American Psychiatric Association. *Diagnostic and Statistical Manual of Mental Disorders.* 4th ed. Washington: American Psychiatric Association, 1994.

Anspaugh, David J., Michael H. Hamrick, and Frank D. Rosato. *Wellness: Concepts and Applications.* St. Louis: Mosby-Year Book, Inc., 1991.

Basini, Richard A. *How to Cut Down Your Social Drinking.* New York: G. P. Putnams Sons, 1985.

Bates, Carson, and James Wigtil. *Skill-Building Activities for Alcohol and Drug Education.* Boston: Jones and Bartlett Publishers, Inc., 1994.

Bell, Tammy L. *Adolescent Relapse Warning Signs.* Independence, MO: Herald House/Independence Press, 1989.

Bilodeau, Lorrainne. *The Anger Workbook.* Minneapolis: CompCare Publishers, 1992.

Bourne, Edmund J. *The Anxiety & Phobia Workbook.* Oakland, CA: New Harbinger Publications, Inc., 1990.

Brill, Naomi I. *Working with People.* 4th ed. New York: Longman, 1990.

Canfield, Jack, and Harold C. Wells. *100 Ways to Enhance Self-concept in the Classroom: A Handbook for Teachers and Parents.* Englewood Cliffs, N.J.: Prentice-Hall, Inc., 1976.

Carnes, Patrick. *A Gentle Path through the Twelve Steps.* Minneapolis: CompCare Publishers, 1993.

Carroll, Charles R. *Drugs in Modern Society.* 3d ed. Madison, Wis: WCB Brown & Benchmark Publishers, 1993.

Cottrell, Randall R. *Wellness: Stress Management.* Guilford, CT: The Dushkin Publishing Group, Inc., 1992.

Davis, Martha, Elizabeth Robbins Eshelman, and Matthew McKay. *The Relaxation & Stress Reduction Workbook.* 3d ed. Oakland, CA: New Harbinger Publications, Inc., 1988.

Dugan, Timothy F., and Robert Coles, eds. *The Child in our Times.* New York: Brunner/Mazel, Inc., 1989.

Elias, Maurice J., and Steven E. Tobias. *Problem Solving/ Decision Making.* National Education Association of the United States, 1990.

Ellis, Dave. *Becoming a Master Student.* 7th ed. Boston: Houghton Mifflin Company, 1994.

Federal Bureau of Prisons. *Understanding Substance Abuse & Treatment.* Washington, D.C., 1992.

Gerne, Patricia J., and Timothy A. Gerne, Jr. *Substance Abuse Prevention Activities For Secondary Students.* Englewood Cliffs, N.J.: Prentice Hall, 1991.

Goldenberg, Irene, and Herbert Goldenberg. *My Self in Family Context.* Belmont, CA, 1991.

Goode, Erich. *Drugs in American Society.* 4th ed. New York: McGraw-Hill, Inc., 1993.

Gorski, Terence T. *Addictive Relationships: Why Love Goes Wrong in Recovery.* Independence, MO: Herald House/Independence Press, 1993.

Gorski, Terence T. *The Staying Sober Workbook.* rev. ed. Independence, MO: Herald House/Independence Press, 1992.

Greenberg, Jerrold S. *Your Personal Stress Profile and Activity Workbook.* Dubuque, IA: Wm. C. Brown Publishers, 1992.

Hazelden. *Refusal Skills.* Center City, MN: Hazelden Foundation, 1993.

———. *Treating The Cocaine Abuser*, by David E. Smith, M.D. and Donald R. Wesson, M.D. Center City, MN: Hazelden Foundation, 1985.

———. *Understanding Major Anxiety Disorders and Addiction*, by Ihsan M. Salloum, M.D., and Dennis C. Daley. Center City, MN: Hazelden Foundation, 1994.

———. *Hope and Recovery - The Workbook.* Minneapolis, MN: CompCare Publishers, 1990.

Inaba, Darryl S., and William E. Cohen. *Uppers, Downers, All Arounders.* 2d. ed. Ashland, OR: CNS Productions, Inc., 1993.

Insel, Paul M., and Walton T. Roth. *Core Concepts in Health.* 7th ed. Mountain View, CA: Mayfield Publishing Company, 1994.

Institute for Substance Abuse Research. *Drugs of Abuse Digest.* 9th ed. Vero Beach, FL, 1993.

Jackson, Tom. *Activities That Teach.* Cedar City, UT, 1993.

Jones, Lee, and Victoria Kimbrough. *Great Ideas.* New York: Cambridge University Press, 1987.

Krause, Carol. *How Healthy Is Your Family Tree?* New York: Fireside, 1995.

Kinney, Jean, and Swen Leaton. *Loosening the Grip.* 4th ed. St. Louis: Mosby-Year Book, Inc., 1991.

Lewis, Judith A., Robert Q. Dana, and Gregory A. Blevins. *Substance Abuse Counseling.* 2d. ed. Pacific Grove, CA: Brooks/Cole Publishing Company, 1994.

Liska, Ken. *Drugs and the Human Body with Implications for Society.* 4th ed. New York: Macmillan Publishing Company, 1990.

Lowinson, Joyce H., Pedro Ruiz, and Robert Millman. *Substance Abuse: A Comprehensive Textbook.* 2d. ed. Baltimore: Williams & Wilkins, 1992.

Lohman, Keith D. *Drugs and Alcohol: The Big Questions and Ideas for Prevention.* New York: McGraw-Hill, Inc., 1994.

McKay, Matthew, and Patrick Fanning. *Self-Esteem.* Oakland, CA: New Harbinger Publications, 1987.

McKay, Matthew, Martha Davis, and Patrick Fanning. *Thoughts & Feelings: The Art of Cognitive Stress Intervention.* Richmond, CA: New Harbinger Publications, 1981.

Meeks, Linda, Philip Heit, and Randy Page. *Violence Prevention.* Blacklick, OH: Meeks Heit Publishing Company, Inc., 1995.

Miller, Merlene, and Terence T. Gorski. *Lowering the Risk*. Independence, MO: Herald House/Independence Press, 1991.

Moore, Thomas. *Care Of The Soul*. New York: HarperCollins Publishers, Inc., 1992.

National Research Council. *Preventing Drug Abuse*. Washington, D.C.: National Academy Press, 1993.

Oregon Prevention Resource Center. *A Guide to Self-Help Groups for Alcohol and Drug Addiction*. Salem, OR. 1991.

Palladino, Connie. *Developing Self-Esteem: A Positive Guide For Personal Success*. Los Altos, CA: Crisp Publications, Inc., 1989.

Payne, Wayne A., Dale B. Hahn, and Robert R. Pinger. *Drugs: Issues for Today*. St. Louis, MO: Mosby-Year Book, Inc., 1991.

Pita, Dianne Doyle. *Addictions Counseling*. New York: The Crossroad Publishing Company, 1994.

Presley, Cheryl A., Philip W. Meilman, and Rob Lyerla. *Use, Consequences, and Perceptions of the Campus Environment*. Vol 1, *Alcohol and Drugs on American College Campuses*. Carbondale, IL: The Core Institute, 1993.

Ray, Oakley and Charles Ksir. *Drugs, Society & Human Behavior*. 6th ed. St. Louis, MO: Mosby-Year Book, Inc., 1993.

Remington, Dennis, Garth Fisher, and Edward Parent. *How To Lower Your Fat Thermostat*. Provo, UT: Vitality House International, Inc., 1983.

Rice, Phillip L. *Stress And Health: Principles and Practice for Coping and Wellness*. Monterey, CA: Brooks/Cole Publishing Company, 1987.

Roche, Helena. *The Addiction Process: From Enabling to Intervention*. Deerfield Beach, FL: Health Communications, Inc., 1990.

Schlaadt, Richard G. *Alcohol Use & Abuse*. Guilford, CT: The Dushkin Publishing Group, Inc., 1992.

———*Drugs, Society & Behavior*. Guilford, CT: The Dushkin Publishing Group, Inc., 1992.

Springhouse Corporation. *Physicians Drug Handbook*. 5th ed. Springhouse, PA., n.d.

Stanford, Gene and Albert E. Roark. *Human Interaction In Education*. Boston: Allyn and Bacon, Inc., 1974.

Travis, John W. and Regina Sara Ryan. *The Wellness Workbook*. 2d.ed. Berkeley: Ten Speed Press, 1988.

U.S. Congress. Office of Technology Assessment. *Technologies for Understanding and Preventing Substance Abuse and Addiction*. n.d.

U.S. Congress. House. Committee on Energy and Commerce. Subcommittee on Health and the Environment. *Advertising of Tobacco Products*. 99th Cong., 2d sess., 1986. Serial 99-167.

———. *Hearings on Tobacco Advertising*. 100th Cong., 1st sess., 1987. Serial 100-20.

———. Subcommittee on Oversight and Investigations. *Cigarette Advertising and the HHS Anti-Smoking Campaign*. 97th Cong., 1st sess., 1981. Serial 97-66.

———. Subcommittee on Telecommunications, Consumer Protection, and Finance. *Beer and Wine Advertising: Impact of Electronic Media*. 99th Cong., 1st sess., 1985. Serial 99-16.

———. Subcommittee on Transportation and Hazardous Materials. *Tobacco Issues*. 101st Cong., 1st sess., 1989. pts. 1 and 2. Serial 101-85 and 101-126.

———. Subcommittee on Transportation, Tourism, and Hazardous Materials. *Cigarettes: Advertising, Testing, and Liability*. 100th Cong., 2d sess., 1988. Serial 100-217.

U.S. Congress. House. Select Committee on Children, Youth, and Families. *Confronting the Impact of Alcohol Labeling and Marketing on Native American Health and Culture*. 102d Cong., 2d sess., 1992.

———. *Preventing Underage Drinking: A Dialogue with the Surgeon General*. 102d Cong., 1st sess., 1991.

U.S. Congress. Senate. Committee on Commerce, Science, and Transportation. Subcommittee on Consumer. *Alcohol Beverage Advertising Act, S.664*. 102d Cong., 2d sess., 1992.

———. *The Sensible Advertising and Family Education Act, S.674*. 103rd Cong., 1st sess., 1993.

———.*Tobacco Product Education and Health Protection Act of 1991*. S.1088. 102d Cong., 1st sess., 1991.

U.S. Congress. Senate. Committee on Labor and Human Resources. Subcommittee on Children, Family, Drugs, and Alcoholism. *Alcohol Advertising*. 99th Cong., 1st sess., 1985.

———. Committee on the Judiciary. *Hearing on Domestic Violence*. 103rd Cong., 1st sess., 1993. Serial J-103-2.

———. Committee on Labor and Human Resources. *Tobacco Product Education and Health Protection Act of 1990*. 101st Cong., 2d sess., 1990. S 1883. pts. 1 and 2.

U.S. Department of Education. *Alcohol and Other Drugs.*, n.d.

———*Learning to Live Drug Free*. Washington, D.C., n.d.

U.S. Department of Health and Human Services. National Institutes of Health. *Alcohol and Interpersonal Violence: Fostering Multidisciplinary Perspectives*. Research Monograph no. 24. NIH Publication no. 93-3496. Rockville, MD, 1993.

———. National Institute on Alcohol Abuse and Alcoholism. *Prevention Plus: Involving Schools, Parents, and the Community in Alcohol and Drug Education*. DHHS Publication no. (ADM) 83-1256. Washington: Government Printing Office, 1983.

——. *Planning a Prevention Program.* Publication no. (ADM) 281-75-0013. Rockville, MD, 1977.

——. National Institute on Drug Abuse. *Cue Extinction: In-Service Training Curriculum.* NIH Publication no. 993-3692. Rockville, MD, 1993.

——. *Addicted Women: Family Dynamics, Self Perceptions, and Support Systems.* DHEW Publication no. (ADM) 80-762. Rockville, MD, 1979.

——. *Drug Abuse Prevention Research.* DHHS Publication no. (ADM) 83-1270. Rockville, MD, 1993.

——. *Drugs And Crime.* Research Issues 17. DHEW Publication no. (ADM) 77-393. Rockville, MD, 1976.

——. *Drugs and Violence: Causes, Correlates, and Consequences.* NIDA Research Monograph 103. Rockville, MD, 1990.

——. *Drug Abuse Prevention Intervention Research: Methodical Issues.* NIDA Research Monograph 107. Rockville, MD, 1991.

——. *Drug Abuse Among Minority Youth: Methodological Issues and Recent Research Advances.* NIDA Research Monograph 130. Rockville, MD, 1993.

——. *Etiology of Drug Abuse: Implications for Prevention.* NIDA Research Monograph 56. Rockville, MD, 1985.

——. *Treatment Services for Drug Dependent Women.* Vol. II. DHHS Publication no. 82-1219. Rockville, MD, 1982.

——. *Perspectives on the History of Psychoactive Substance Use.* Research Issues 24. DHEW Publication no. (ADM) 79-810. Rockville, MD, 1979.

——. *Preventing Adolescent Drug Abuse: Intervention Strategies.* NIDA Research Monograph 47. Rockville, MD, 1983.

——. *Prevention Research: Deterring Drug Abuse Among Children and Adolescents.* NIDA Research Monograph 63. Rockville, MD, 1985.

——. *Women And Drugs.* Research Issues 31. DHHS Publication no. (ADM) 83-1268. Rockville, MD, 1983.

——. *Women and Drugs: A New Era for Research.* NIDA Research Monograph 65. Rockville, MD, 1986.

——. Office for Substance Abuse Prevention. *Alcohol Practices, Policies, and Potentials of American Colleges and Universities.* An OSAP White Paper by Lewis D. Eigen. Rockville, MD, 1991.

——. *National Survey Results on Drug Use from The Monitoring The Future Study, 1975-1993. Vol. I. Secondary School Students.* NIH Publication no. 94-3809. Washington: Government Printing Office, 1994.

——. *National Survey Results on Drug Use from The Monitoring The Future Study, 1975-1993. Vol. II. College Students and Young Adults.* NIH Publication no. 94-3810. Washington: GPO, 1994.

——. *Prevention Plus II: Tools for Creating and Sustaining Drug-Free Communities.* DHHS Publication no. (ADM) 89-11649. Rockville, MD, 1989.

——. *Prevention Plus III: Assessing Alcohol and Other Drug Prevention Programs at the School and Community Level.* DHHS Publication no. (ADM) 91-1817. Rockville, MD, 1991.

——. *Proceedings of a National Conference on Preventing Alcohol and Drug Abuse in Black Communities.* May 22-24, 1987. Washington, D.C. DHHS Publication no. (ADM) 89-1648. Rockville, MD, 1990.

——. *Youth and Drugs: Society's Mixed Messages.* OSAP Prevention Monograph-6. DHHS Publication no. (ADM) 90-1689. Rockville, MD, 1990.

——. Substance Abuse and Mental Health Services Administration. *National Household Survey on Drug Abuse: Population Estimates 1993.* DHHS Publication no. (SMA) 94-3017. Rockville, MD, 1994.

——. *Children: Getting a Head Start Against Drugs. Teacher's Guide* by Sylvia Carter and Ura Jean Oyemade. DHHS Publication no. (SMA)93-1970. 1993.

——. *Parents: Getting a Head Start Against Drugs. Activity Book.* Authored by Sylvia Carter and Ura Jean Oyemade. DHHS Publication no. (SMA)93-1971. 1993.

——. *Parents: Getting a Head Start Against Drugs. Trainer's Guide.* Authored by Sylvia Carter and Ura Jean Oyemade. DHHS Publication no. (SMA)93-1971. 1993.

——. *Signs of Effectiveness II. Preventing Alcohol, Tobacco, and Other Drug Use: A Risk Factor/Resiliency-Based Approach.* DHHS Publication no. (SAM) 94-2098. 1994.

U.S. General Accounting Office. Committee on Education and Labor, House of Representatives. Report to the Chairman, Subcommittee on Select Education. *Adolescent Drug Use Prevention.* PEMD-92-2.

Western Regional Center for Drug-Free Schools and Communities. *Turning The Corner: From Risk to Resiliency.* Portland, OR: Northwest Regional Educational Library, 1993.

Weston Woods Institute. *Counseling Children of Alcoholics: Fostering Resiliency.* Weston, CT: The Media Group of Connecticut, Inc., 1994.

Witters, Weldon, Peter Venturelli, and Glen Hanson. *Drugs and Society.* 3d. ed. Boston: Jones and Bartlett Publishers, 1992.

World Health Organization. *Preventing and Controlling Drug Abuse.* Geneva: WHO, 1990.